Hints for Success in School

A Practical Guide for Students

By Joe Deely

NEW FORUMS

NEW FORUMS PRESS INC.

Published in the United States of America
by New Forums Press, Inc.1018 S. Lewis St.
Stillwater, OK 74074
www.newforums.com

Library of Congress Cataloging-in-Publication Data Pending

This book may be ordered in bulk quantities at discount from New Forums Press, Inc., P.O. Box 876, Stillwater, OK 74076 [Federal I.D. No. 73 1123239]. Printed in the United States of America.

ISBN 10: 1-58107-312-7
ISBN 13: 978-1-58107-312-6

Testimonials

"*Hints for Success in School* is a great read not only for student but parents alike. The practical rational for every step is easy to ingest and implement. Joe's easy sense of humor and practicality, both combine for a perfect plan for success. As a high school counselor, I will no doubt both use strategies found inside but, also forward on this book to my students and parents to assist in increasing success in school. Joe is not only a great person but one of the best teachers a child could have."

Doug Reimondo
M.S. Ed , School Counselor

"Joseph Deely's *Hints for Success* are practical, easy to understand, and get right to the point. All students (and teachers and parents too) can look through these hints to find ones that can help them. If you're already successful in school, read through the hints and pat yourself on the back when you recognize what you're doing right. I'll use Joe's hints to help students improve their goal setting and self-affirmation skills."

Mark Hopkins
M.A.Ed., Special Education Teacher, New York State

"Using an armada of unique life and classroom experiences to ignite his inspirational, thought-provoking prose, Deely has crafted an engrossing book that will leave readers of all ages and abilities with a long list of quality tips for modern-day academic success."

Paul Smartschan
Library Media Specialist, XC & Indoor Track Coach,
Assistant Soccer Coach, Powhatan High School

"A wonderful insight into the lives of students in the classroom. Thought provoking and truly motivating!"

Sharon Faubert
Attendance Officer, Coordinator of Adult Education

"Mr. Deely's *Hints for Success* stands out as a relevant and interesting read for students in a sea of otherwise mundane student guides. The book is written in a pragmatic style that will keep the reader engaged. Mr. Deely's real life experiences and care for student success transfers beautifully to the text in a friendly and caring voice. A must read for students of all backgrounds and levels of success."

Dr. Michael J. Massa
High School Principal

Table of Contents

Introduction ix
Acknowledgments xi
Section 1 - Hints Students Can Be Successful
   at Today 1
- Section introduction......................................2
  1 Never take a zero 3
  2 Get involved at school 5
  3 Read directions.......................................7
  4 Use gizmos to help.................................9
  5 Do any extra credit............................... 11
  6 Look at illustrations first 13
  7 Ask questions 15
  8 Participate in class................................17
  9 Be polite toward others 19
 10 Challenge yourself................................21

Section 2 - Hints That Change Bad Habits
   into Good Habits 23
  - Section introduction 24
  1 Have your materials ready for class......25
  2 Be on time to class 27
  3 Do hard work first 29
  4 Use your time wisely 31
  5 List assignments in your planners........33
  6 Develop a growth vs. a fixed mindset...35
  7 Keep your binder and book bag neat 37
  8 Be attentive in class 39
  9 Do work the day you get it....................41
 10 Edit your writing assignments 43
 11 No excuses - No one wants to hear them.............45

Section 3 - Hints That You Can Work On Outside of School..47
- Section introduction...48
1 Get your sleep 49
2 Get a job 51
3 Look and dress the part..53
4 Read as much as you can 55
5 Post your goals..57
6 Eat a healthy diet..59
7 Use short study session with rewards 61
8 Don't study things you already know 63
9 Set aside quiet time each day.................................65
10 Study for tests 67
11 Do your homework 69
12 Complete your assignment & turn work in...........71

Section 4 - Hints That Require Internal Change ...73
- Section introduction...74
1 Never give up..75
2 Avoid drama 77
3 Get your exercise 79
4 Be passionate about your hobbies..........................81
5 Take pride in your work 83
6 Avoid multitasking 85
7 Look forward to changes 87
8 Have fun in school 89
9 he future is now...91
10 Discover your passions and follow them..............93
11 Take creative chances..95
12 Your grades - Your report card..............................97

**Section 5 - Hints That Require Some Help
from Others** **99**
- Section introduction.. 100
1 Seek adult help.. 101
2 Avoid drugs 103
3 See teacher ASAP for makeup work.................. 105
4 Find a mentor to talk to about grades................. 107
5 Get a study buddy 109
6 Get tutoring help 111
7 Attend review sessions for standardized tests.... 113
8 Hang out with smart people 115
9 Imitate positive role models.............................. 117

Section 6 - Hints That May Take a While **119**
- Section introduction.. 120
1 Avoid bad students 121
2 Maintain a positive attitude............................... 123
3 Care about your G.P.A. 125
4 Be honest and have integrity.............................. 127
5 When you get down - get busy........................... 129
6 Take a fun class each semester........................... 131
7 Never sell yourself short 133
8 Don't beat yourself up when you fail.................. 135
9 Attack your weaknesses 137
10 Think of school as an opportunity to learn 139
11 Be your own hero – No one else will.................. 141

Last Thoughts..**143**
About the Author **145**

Introduction

"Nothing in the world can take the place of persistence. Talent will not; nothing is more common than unsuccessful men with talent. Genius will not; unrewarded genius is almost a proverb. Education will not; the world is full of educated derelicts. Persistence and determination alone are omnipotent. The slogan Press On! Has solved and always will solve the problems of the human race."
                              Calvin Coolidge

If you like what you do you'll never have to work a day in your life and someone will still pay you for your time.
                              Joseph E. Deely, Jr.

Not all the hints in this collection will work for everyone. Batman's belt has a lot of devices and depending on the need that arises he is able to pull from these gadgets to aid him in his crime fighting. These hints are to students what the gizmos on the bat belt are like for the Dark Knight. While not every hint will work well for everyone, hopefully there are a few in this collection that may come in handy for students to use to improve their grades. Students will have to decide which piece of advice will work for them. After reading this guide if one grade in one semester goes up a letter I'll be happy for you and consider that an improvement. Changing things for the better takes baby steps. While these small individual steps at times may not seem important, if applied and practiced they start to build a pattern of good habits that can help students achieve success in school and beyond.
                              JD

Acknowledgements

**"When you practice gratefulness, there is a sense
of respect toward others."**
Dalai Lama

Many people have helped with seeing this book come to print. I am thankful to my in-laws, Dave Ridenour and Patricia L'Herrou, for their editing help and wonderful words of encouragement. I'm thankful to several colleagues who took the time to read the book and write nice reviews. These educators include: Sharon Faubert, Chris Garland, Dr. Michael Massa, Doug Reimondo, and Paul Smartschan. Michelle Martin is a wiz on computers and was very helpful on technical formatting – thank you. For letting me bend an ear on many issues, I'm thankful for my longtime friend and fellow teacher Mark Hopkins, who is always a phone call away. A big thanks to Maryvel Firda who helped me to ask the right questions about publishing. A huge thank you to my publisher, Douglas Dollar and the good people at New Forums Press for the many things that they do. My wife, Maile L'Herrou, who gives me her honest opinions and who is always helpful and encouraging – thank you. Lastly, I'm thankful to my students who, through their successes and failures, have inspired this book.

Many Thanks, JD

Section 1 - Hints Students Can be Successful at Today

- Section introduction...2
1 Never take a zero 3
2 Get involved at school 5
3 Read directions..7
4 Use gizmos to help..9
5 Do any extra credit..11
6 Look at illustrations first 13
7 Ask questions 15
8 Participate in class...17
9 Be polite toward others 19
10 Challenge yourself...21

Hints Students Can Be Successful at Today

I enjoy checking off goals that are relativity easy to accomplish. Dropping off the mail, going to the bank, checking the air in the tires, doing the dishes are all tasks that are fairly simple to complete and necessary for a smooth day. I will find, however, that even the most mundane tasks can seem arduous if my day gets busy with a lot of daily assignments. It seems that if I'm able to finish some of the easy jobs on my to do list it gets the ball rolling and it serves to provide me with a small sense of accomplishment that helps me to get other more important things finished.

In this section students are presented with hints that they can start using immediately. These are the hints that students may want to attempt first because they are more likely to experience immediate successes. This group can be viewed as more short term, or seen as slight changes in practice for a student's daily routine. These simpler hints when accomplished and mastered can do a lot for a student's overall success and help boost their confidence for tackling other hints that may be harder to achieve.

P.S. Always attempt to build on your successes no matter how small.

#1 Never Take a Zero

"Sometimes one pays most for the things one gets for nothing."
Albert Einstein

Getting your name associated with zero can be one of the most shameful things a person could achieve. Unfortunately for many students taking a zero on any given assignment is deemed acceptable. Leaving a blank next to any academic question can only result in a zero, and zeros can only result in failure.

I have had plenty of students in the past who have failed class not because they were dumb but because they simple did not turn in assignments. It was not that they could not do the work, they just didn't. However, I've had numerous students over the years who may not have been blessed with terrific aptitude, but were able to overcome their lack of ability through effort and determination. Students who never take a zero have learned one of the basic principles of success, which is doing all your work.

Failing an assignment is never good but it does supply you with points towards an overall grade. Example:

	Student A	**Student B**
Assignment # 1	20/20	20/20
Assignment # 2	20/20	20/20
Assignment # 3	**13/20**	**0/20**
Assignment # 4	20/20	20/20
	73/80 = **91%**	60/80 = **75%**

Both students above failed assignment # 3, however student A did turn in the assignment and received points, while student B failed to turn in the assignment and took a zero. The result is a 16% difference in their grades all based on just one assignment.

Try this: For the next ten days at school complete every assignment and turn everything in, then check with your teachers and see how that has positively affected your grade. If you want to take it another step then work with your teachers and go back and complete any assignments that you did not finish from earlier in the grading period. Don't take zeros!

#2 Get Involved at School

"The quality of moral behavior varies in inverse ratio to the number of human beings involved."
Aldous Huxley

One of my favorite things to do as a teacher is to attend the end of the year awards assembly. At this gathering students are recognized and rewarded for their years of hard work and dedication to their studies. Many students leave the assembly with honors and dozens exit with scholarships they will use to further their educational pursuits. Invariably these top students at school are always involved in extracurricular activities. They are members of the band. They take part in athletics. They are involved with student government. They are in clubs.

More often than not students who fail seem to never participate in any of the activities their schools have to offer. This lack of participation is not always the fault of the student. Parents may be unable or unwilling to sign permission forms, get their children physicals for athletics, or drive them to extracurricular activities. Students may not take part in school related activities because of many reasons, such as: lack of confidence, hatred of school, or complete disinterest. Whatever the reasoning may be, student who don't get involved don't get ahead. Students who don't get involved at school experience less exposure to interpersonal skills that are essential to positive growth and healthy relationships.

While some sports teams at school have cuts many

do not. Often anyone is allowed to join athletic teams. Schools that offer clubs are usually open to all students. Schools often participate in fund raising activities and student volunteers are always needed. Whether it's helping out with a canned food drive, giving blood, or running in a 5K, students are always needed, encouraged, and welcomed to take part.

Try this: Join one of the many clubs that your school may offer. This can be done at any time of the school year. Look and listen for announcements of volunteer activities. Students are always needed. Take part, take charge, and get involved.

#3 Read Directions

"Education is when you read the fine print. Experience is what you get if you don't."
Pete Seeger

If you were alive in the 1970s and had a father that attempted to assemble a back yard metal swing set without reading the directions you might understand the importance of this hint. Needless to say it would of save a great bit of time and several curse words if he had taken the time to read the instructions. Good students take the time to read the instructions because they have learned that by doing so they gain an advantage into exactly what is expected from them on each particular task. Reading and understanding directions is the first step towards correctly answering questions. Students who read directions have formed a habit that will ultimately save them a good deal of time and a lot of grief.

Unfortunately, many students don't take the time to read the instructions on a test. A prime example is the directions for the short essay section I have given on an English test. The directions are as follows: **Pick any 3 of the 5 following essays to answer**. Every year a few students struggle to write all five essays, this even after I had reminded the students to read the directions.

You wouldn't sign a business contract without first reading what you are agreeing to. You wouldn't play a new board game without first reading the rules, yet students will often jump into taking a test without a glance at what the directions instruct them to specifically do. Students who fail often do so because they are in the poor habit of skipping as much work as possible. These students will often attempt to do the minimum amount of work necessary just to get through something without a care towards the accuracy of their answers.

Try this: Take the time to read any direction that your instructors give. Your directions may be at the beginning of a section on a test, on the board, or on your computer screen. Read all directions and before you proceed make sure you have a clear understanding of what is expected of you. Never assume you know what is necessary until you read all the directions.

#4 Use Gizmos to Help

"We've arranged a civilization in which most crucial elements profoundly depend on science and technology."

Carl Sagan

As a kid in school if the teacher gave us free reading time I used to love pulling an encyclopedia from the book case and randomly start leafing through it. In a world before classroom computers the encyclopedia was the greatest source of concentrated knowledge available to me growing up. Today students have a plethora of sources to access information from. Good students learn to acquire data they need by using their phone, computer pad, or any number of other gizmos on the market that can access information. While these educational tools are nice to have, they can be expensive and many students are limited because of the financial issues in their families and school districts.

By using our current technology students can learn to pronounce words correctly, see teachers on video working out math problems, get definitions in science, and learn history facts. Chemistry labs, music scales, cooking recipes, and any number of "how to" discoveries are readily available through the use of technology that many kids have in their pockets. Being wise is not about knowledge you have, it's about the ability to find the answers you seek.

Most people seek out technology gadgets not as a device to gain knowledge but as a source of entertainment. While playing games and checking out the many social media websites can be seen as enjoyable, they also foster addictions and are often a complete waste of time. Many students who fail at school experience success in killing the most goblins, seeing videos of celebrities making fools of themselves, or finding out who is doing what at school. While these students may get the high score in a video game or know the latest bit of gossip at school, it does very little to help them achieve academic success in the game of life.

Try this: If you have a smart phone, install some basic educational applications. See web based tutorial videos to help with concepts you are having trouble understanding. Seek out any of the many technological avenues that will help you gain knowledge. Try to avoid the entertainment sites that waste your time.

#5 Do Any Extra Credit

"It's never crowded along the extra mile."
Wayne Dyer

"The difference between ordinary and extraordinary is that little extra."
Jimmy Johnson

Perhaps one of the hardest things for me to see as a teacher are students passing up the opportunity to easily get better scores on assignments. Seeing a student skip extra credit questions on tests just so they can be finished faster make me want to throttle them. Extra credit is a gift and students who want to do well accept it and use it to their advantage. Some students will even ask for any extra work because they understand that any extra effort they put into a class the better the reward is at the end.

Students who don't succeed often reject any opportunity to do extra work that could help their grades. Extra credit is offered by teachers to help students who are struggling boost their grades. However, teachers will tell you the majority of students who take advantage of extra credit aren't the at-risk students, rather it's the students who are already doing well and want to excel. Failing students seldom complete regular assignments, so to offer them extra work is a bit like offering additional shifts to an employee who does a lousy job in the first place.

Consider the following example:

Student	Pts. Earned/ Total Pts.	Extra Pts.	Final Pts. Total
Mary	744/1000	57	811/1000
Ann	744/1000	Did Not Do	744/1000

Both students had the same base point totals; however Mary ended up with an 81%. Ann did not take advantage of the few extra points that where available to her and received a 74%. This letter grade difference may eventually lead to helping Mary get into college or receiving a scholarship.

Try this: For the next two weeks do any extra credit problems or assignments for class. Ask all your teachers if there is any extra work you can do to help boost your grades. Take the extra step and climb a little higher.

#6 Look at Illustrations First

Number of hints followed

G.P.A.	0	10	20	30	40	50	60	70	80	90
4.00					.		. . .		.. .	.
3.50				.		.	.		.	
3.00			.		. .					
2.50		.. .		.						
2.00		. .	.							
1.50	. .									
1.00	. .									
0.50	..									
0.00										

Students = .

"As you can see by this chart, following more hints improves your grades!" J.D.

Although some subjects lend themselves more towards illustrations than others, every educational discipline can feature some form of visual learning. Graphs, charts, time lines, and even cartoons are often used on standardized and teacher generated tests. Students who have the ability to grasp the understanding of illustrations will consistently do better on most tests. The best approach to tackling these types of questions is to look at the illustrations *first* before reading any question. Once you understand the meaning of an illustration it is usually much easier to extrapolate any answer you will need.

Students who attempt to answer these problems starting from the questions are at a disadvantage because they have not first viewed the illustration and begun to understand the concept of what the graph, chart, or picture is relaying. Attempting to answer a question by reading the options of possible choices first is like driving into an unfamiliar intersection without consulting a map to help guide you to where you need to go. It will take extra time to study the map, but it will help you get to your destination with less hassle and more accuracy.

Try this: The next time you have a test that uses any type of illustrations study the illustrations before you attempt to read the corresponding questions. This approach will take a little longer but you'll be pleased with your results.

#7 Ask Questions

"The art and science of asking questions is the source of all knowledge."
Thomas Berger

I have to honestly admit that after 20 years of teaching I never once had a student ask me a question I didn't like. I suppose that tells me I must be in the right career field. While teaching I've had many serious questions, some questions I had to tell the students I didn't know the answer to, a few personal questions which I gracefully sidestepped, but in all my years I never had a student ask a stupid question. I'm not even sure if there is such a thing as a stupid question. How can trying to find the correct answer to anything be stupid?

Good students come to realize that if they engage themselves in class by actively asking questions they not only get more out of lessons, they also learn skills of interaction that later become important when they enter the work force. Often participation counts as part of a grade in many classes. Students who ask questions in class will generally have much better grades than those who sit in the back row not contributing. When students are involved they discover that class time seems to go by fast because they are a participant and not just an inactive spectator.

Teachers rely on student interaction to help them tailor the instructional needs of the class. Perhaps the worst class is one in which the students don't ask any questions. In these classes it can feel like attempting to teach in a morgue. Nothing is more frustrating than trying to teach kids who are disengaged. The student, who just sits in class and is not interested in anything because he has completely tuned out, is one of the most difficult types of kids to reach because they are not giving teachers any feedback.

Try this: Start raising your hand and ask questions in class. Become an active part of your learning environment. You may discover that you will enjoy your classes more and your grades will naturally go up.

#8 Participate in Class

"One of the penalties for refusing to participate in politics is that you end up being governed by your inferiors."

Plato

One of the things I was always good about doing as a student was to participate in class. I was lucky because talking came naturally to me and I never felt too shy or inhibited about sharing my feelings on topics or asking questions. I discovered the more I interacted in class, the more I was able to get out of a subject. Getting involved in class is perhaps the most important thing a student can do to help aid them in their understanding of a topic.

Many teachers tie class participation into part of their curriculum. As a student having a percent of my grade come from class participation was like getting a gift that helped to balance any points I was bound to lose on tests or projects. Good students, even the shy ones, will see that participation in class is one of the easiest ways to increase your grade. One simple method of participating is to ask questions in class. Educators love questions and being asked their opinions on issues. It only makes sense that teachers will look fondly on those students who take the time to ask questions.

Weaker students, for many different reasons, have a tendency to disengage themselves from being an integral part of their classroom learning environment. While these students may still do well in class, more often than not those who remain silent will struggle with new concepts and fail to comprehend topic discussions. When a person speaks they want to sound smart, so engaging in participation requires some forethought as to what will come across as sounding intelligent and meaningful. Unfortunately many students are not willing to think and interact with their classes.

Try this: For the next week really make an effort to be more involved in class discussions. Raise your hand, asked questions, and take an active role in your learning. See if your attitude about the class changes when you make yourself a more important member of the class. Take part!

#9 Be Polite Towards Others

"Be as polite to the custodian as you are to the chairman of the board."

H. Jackson Brown Jr.

This might sound like a rule you might see posted in a kindergarten class, but it no longer surprises me that many students, even at the secondary and college levels, still lack the basic practices of common politeness. One of the most important aspects of being successful is having the ability to get along well with others. Colleagues at work who seem to connect with the widest range of people are often leaders and frequently excel in many aspects of their job. A common theme of their success seems to be that these people are consistently polite towards others. The best students are often the ones who not only do well academically but are pleasant to be around because they show kindness towards others.

During my past 20 years of teaching I've had an assortment of difficult students who have been in my classes. It seems that many of these students who have been at risk to graduate arc also the same ones who seem to have issues with understanding the powerful advantages of being polite. These students often are unaware of the generally accepted courtesies that are common among most of their peers. Many of these kids come from families that never taught them how to be polite. Their absence of manners comes across as having a difficult attitude, which often leads them to getting in trouble with other students and with teachers. While teachers and administrators are some of the most patient people in the world, it is always easier to help students who are struggling when they are nice. It is at the core of human nature to help those who show kindness in return as opposed to those who simply are rude and hard to get along with.

Try this: For the next week practice being kind to others. Use the phrase, "Thank you," more often and always attempt to be as polite as you can towards everyone. Remember, being kind doesn't cost a thing and you might discover that it really helps in relationships with your peers and teachers.

#10 Challenge Yourself

"When we meet real tragedy in life, we can react in two ways - either by losing hope and falling into self-destructive habits, or by using the challenge to find our inner strength."
                                    Dalai Lama

"The ultimate measure of a man is not where he stands in moments of comfort and convenience, but where he stands at times of challenge and controversy."
                            Martin Luther King Jr.

Students who have personal drive are the kids who will succeed the most in school because they view challenges not as drudgery, but as opportunities to learn and excel. They have learned to set individual goals for themselves and they put in the extra efforts required to accomplish the tasks needed to reach their desires. They possess the extra spark of gumption it takes to go the additional mile and to do things correctly. Through self-challenges these students pressure themselves to achieve.

There are different ways students learn to be motivated. Often parents, teachers, and coaches can inspire students to be more dedicated to their studies. All students' process inspirational hot buttons that when pushed with correct timing and the right amount of pressure can help influence them towards challenging themselves to accomplish more. The trick for mentors is finding out what these hot buttons are and the timing and pressure of when to push them.

Perhaps the greatest thing that keeps some students from challenging themselves to do more is the fear of failure. These students' view of success is clouded by fears that override their attempts and efforts towards trying to accomplish new things. While some students are just plain lazy, many students that fail are scared of attempting something that might expose them as being inadequate or vulnerable. Few things are as important to most young adults as being able to protect themselves against levels of embarrassment.

Try this: Push yourself to give the extra effort. If you are trying to do 20 sit-ups get to 19 and dig deep and do 6 more. If you are reading a book, add a few more pages to your reading session. If you are learning to play an instrument, increase your practice time. Go the extra mile and challenge yourself to do a little more.

Section 2 - Hints that Change Bad Habits into Good Habits

- Section introduction 24
1 Have your materials ready for class.....................25
2 Be on time to class 27
3 Do hard work first 29
4 Use your time wisely 31
5 List assignments in your planners........................33
6 Develop a growth vs. a fixed mindset..................35
7 Keep your binder and book bag neat 37
8 Be attentive in class 39
9 Do work the day you get it...................................41
10 Edit your writing assignments 43
11 No excuses - No one wants to hear them 45

Hints that Change Bad Habits into Good Habits

Replacing an afternoon snack of a candy bar to that of an apple can really make a big difference in a person's daily health. This may seem like a small thing to convert a candy bar snack to a fruit, but flipping the bad snack to a positive one can begin to pay off. Over time this change of diet can start to pay bigger dividends. On a daily basis we have a tendency not to notice the effects of our poor choices. It is often only after a longer period of time that a person can reflect back and consider the effects of bad choices that could have been positive decisions.

The hints in this section talk about converting bad habits into good ones. All of us have some form of a candy bar for an afternoon snack. What is yours? Is it watching TV too much instead of exercising? Is it texting friends instead of doing your homework? Whatever the candy bar is in your life this section of hints represents those that can change poor habits into positive one.

P.S. What are some of the candy bars in your life?

#1 Have Your Materials Ready for Class

"It's best to have your tools with you. If you don't, you're apt to find something you didn't expect and get discouraged."

Stephen King

This hint may seem like a no brainer, but I am constantly reminded of how important it is to have your materials ready for class. Students who have their necessary materials for class are already a step ahead of several of their peers who come unprepared. If students are well prepared with their materials they will lower their anxiety level because they have less things to worry about and they can better concentrate on learning, which is the whole point of being in class.

I have several students each year that will walk into class with nothing but the clothes on their backs. There are on occasion students, whose families cannot afford the materials, but I have found that the majority of these don't come to class from families that cannot provide; rather, these are students who just don't bother with getting their stuff ready for school. Often these students will interrupt instruction time by asking the teacher or another student for basic necessities such as some paper or a pen. These students start to annoy others because they are perceived as slackers and weak students, which is more than often true. Being unprepared for class is common trait for failing students.

These are a basic list of things a student should have

with them when they walk through the door of most classrooms: Paper, pencils, pens, a calculator, a cell phone, a planner, and books for the class. Hopefully the student will have a type of organizer such as a binder with dividers for each class. All of this should be in a type of backpack, day bag, brief case, valise or some type of bag to help keep all the materials together. Some students will need other items, such as: glasses, hearing aids, cough drops, recording devices, lap tops, and tablets. Football players don't take the field without their helmets on and students shouldn't walk into class without the necessary equipment to learn with.

Try this: For the next week make it a priority to be prepared for each class. It may help to make a list of materials each class requires. At the end of the week do a self-evaluation to see if you were truly ready for each class. Try to make it a habit to always be prepared for class by having the needed materials.

#2 Be on Time to Class

"Arriving late was a way of saying that your own time was more valuable than the time of the person who waited for you."
Karen Joy Fowler

I've been very lucky to have many great students in class during my years of teaching. It seems the best students are those who are always on time and ready to learn. To be asked, *"What are we going to do today?"* has always been one of my favorite questions because it usually comes from an eager student who is in class early and ready to start. It is much better than the kid who strolls in five minutes late with a bad attitude asking, *"Why do we have to do this?"*

Being on time for class is one of the simplest things a student can do to begin the class in the right state of mind. It is one of the best habits a person can acquire not just for school but for every aspect of one's life. Showing up on time is one of the earliest ways we learn responsibility and exhibit respect towards others. Students who are consistently punctual are typically some of the best a teacher will have in class. Being on time shows dependability, which is one of the best character traits a person can possess.

Students who are chronically tardy seem to always suffer academically. Being constantly late speaks volumes about the student's attitude and overall respect level. Being consistently late can lead to attendance referrals and cause the student more academic hassles. Many teachers begin class with a short lesson or some announcements, both of which are critical for students to be on time for. It would be nice if teachers could just fire students who are consistently late. While this option is not open for educators, it is often and easily exercised in the work world for bosses who have employees who are always late.

Try this: For the following two weeks make sure you are on time for everything. Get to class on time. Arrive at appointments when they are scheduled. Don't let anyone have to wait for you for any reason. Also, during this time note how many times you observe other people arriving late to class and other appointments. What thoughts come to mind when you notice people inconveniencing others by being late?

#3 Do Hard Work First

"If it's your job to eat a frog, it's best to do it first thing in the morning. And if it's your job to eat two frogs, it's best to eat the biggest one first."

Mark Twain

It is easy and appealing to do your assignments in the order that pleases you the most. Most students tackle their assignments by doing the work they enjoy more and know they will be successful at accomplishing. The most successful students will turn this approach around. By doing the most difficult tasks first you attack these assignments when your mind is fresh and your motivation to accomplish work is at its greatest level. Students who take the approach of doing the hard work first discover that their grades go up in these subjects.

Failing students are ones that form the bad habit of giving up on difficult work. These students will find any excuse to create a barrier between themselves and their assignments, and they will repeat this approach over and over again. This lack of effort, this give up approach, may be attributed to bad parenting, willful defiance, or just plan laziness. Whatever the case may be, this country is filled with people who achieve nothing because they are unwilling to try. They sell themselves short of their potential and they settle for less than their value.

Students who put off the most difficult assignments are often likely not to finish them or do them incorrectly. Students will find themselves running out of time, lacking energy and motivation when they are facing homework that is difficult. The put off game starts. *"I'll do that in the morning. I'll check with my teacher before class. I'll get to that later this week."* This attitude of procrastination unfortunately becomes a lifelong approach towards tasks that are hard. Not many people enjoy taking the trash out, yet it seems - based off lack of actions - that some must enjoy the fragrance.

Try this: For the next two weeks pick out your most difficult assignments and do them first. See if your grades on these subjects improve. You may even discover that you may start to enjoy these classes more.

#4 Use Your Time Wisely

"I would rather be ashes than dust! I would rather that my spark should burn out in a brilliant blaze than it should be stifled by dry-rot. I would rather be a superb meteor, every atom of me in magnificent glow, than a sleepy and permanent planet. The function of man is to live, not to exist. I shall not waste my days trying to prolong them. I shall use my time."

Jack London

The best students don't waste their time, they get things done. Students who earn good grades are usually on the ball and they take advantage of down time in their day to get things accomplished. As students get older and their lives become more involved with numerous activities, they come to discover that time management is one of their greatest challenges. Students who don't waste time and learn to manage their schedule accomplish more of their goals, achieve a higher level of success, and are generally happier people.

Failing students are typically perpetual time wasters. A common teacher's note on a failing student's report card might read: *Wastes Time in Class.* These students not only waste their own time but they have a tendency to waste the time of others around them. Failing students are like time sponges that absorb the hours of their peers, their teachers, and administrators.

Whether it is worth the effort of the education system

to spend extra resources and time on perpetually failing students is debatable. Ask an educator and their answer should be yes. Ask a parent of a student whose child is in the same class as one of these students and their answer will vary. Ultimately a school systems options to help a failing student becomes restricted as the student progresses in age. By the time failing students get behind in high school they start limiting their educational opportunities. The days of social promotion are virtually over and a diploma of attendance, if available, is not worth the paper it is printed on.

Try this: If you discover a few minutes of down time in a class use that to your advantage. Check your planner, organize your materials, or do a little homework. Get something done! Even if school is not your thing you still have to be there so you might as well make the most of your time. Try to avoid wasting any of your time.

#5 List Assignments in Your Planners

"Organizing is what you do before you do something, so that when you do it, it is not all mixed up."
Alan Alexander Milne

Being well organized is one of the first steps a student can take towards being successful. The most successful students get in the habit of writing down assignments as they get them in each of their classes. By keeping this record it helps the student stay focused on assignments. It helps them to be more responsible while giving the student a visual reminder to help them better organize their time. Keeping records of incoming work and checking off assignments as they are completed gives students a sense of accomplishment.

A well-organized planner that is filled out might look like this:

Class	Subject	Assignment	Due Date
Block 1	Geometry	Page 123 #12-35	Friday (May 1)
Block 2	Health/PE	Fitness Log	Tuesday (May 5)
Block 3	Biology	None	---------
Block 4	English 10	Worksheet	Next class

Students who are consistently behind are often in that position because they fail to remember to do assignments. They hope to rely on their memory or their friends to help remind them what the assignments were as opposed to being a responsible student and writing the assignments down. Poor students will often use the excuse of, *"I forgot to do the work."* Some failing student will actually think that by forgetting to do an assignment it justifies the fact that the work doesn't get done.

Try this: For the next two weeks log all of your homework assignments and projects as you get them in your planner. Check off completed work once you finish each assignment. See if doing this helps you stay better organized and on top of your work.

#6 Develop a Growth vs. Fixed Mindset

"Between stimulus and response there is a space. In that space is our power to choose our response. In our response lies our growth and our freedom."
Viktor E. Frankl

I have often told my students that it is appropriate to say you don't understand something or that you can't do something as long as they follow up that statement with the word *yet*. Good students realize they have an ability to learn and the desire to continue learning. These students ignore the unfavorable inner voice that can often be self-critical. They have developed a *'can do'* attitude that releases them from the bonds that can hold them back. They reject thoughts of negativity and carry an attitude of self-confidence. These are the students that get things done. They can be relied on to work hard and they, more than often, develop into successful people who accomplish many things. Growth demands learning, this requires the gumption to work towards your goals.

The key to developing a growth mindset is to view tasks as positive challenges. The old saying, success breeds success, is absolutely true. When students accomplish difficult tasks it enhances and fosters their abilities to take on even greater goals. Students with growth mindsets develop the habit of viewing school work not as a burden; rather they see it as an avenue towards success, a chance to build self-esteem, and an opportunity to gain knowledge.

Giving up becomes a habit of failing students, which

when practiced releases them from the responsibilities of striving to attempt difficult tasks, thus insuring their success. If they don't try something hard they cannot fail. For instance, if a student doesn't attempt to pronounce a word correctly he'll never mispronounce anything. Many students lack the courage to go out on a limb and be wrong because they are often afraid to be seen as dumb. Unfortunately for these students they have throttled their growth and stifled their potential. Having a fixed mindset develops into a self-fulfilling prophecy of not being smart enough, not being able to, and accepting inadequate performance.

Try this: For the next week try to track your attitude towards new information. Ask yourself if you are responding in a way that can help you move forward or does your mindset keep you stagnated?

#7 Keep Your Binder and Book Bag Neat

"Electricity is really just organized lightning."
George Carlin

Most of the best students I've taught over the years have had one thing in common - they are organized. These students have learned to keep materials they receive in class together in an organized manner. This helps them be better prepared for their classes. Their backpacks are not cluttered with superfluous materials that are unrelated to school. They keep their binders neat and have class work separated for each of their courses. Through keeping their materials well organized they have made themselves ready for classes because they have laid the foundation to receive information. They are prepared to learn.

One of the first things I do when getting a new student is have them clean out their backpack and organize their binder. It is amazing the amount of unneeded materials that some students will carry around with them for months. On several occasions when helping students clean up their binders we will discover old assignments that are completed but were never turned in to teachers. Students may resist doing this at first, but I have found they are generally happier after seeing the stack of old materials they won't have to carry around any longer.

Student who fail often have not learned basic organizational skills that are necessary for being prepared for classes. While they may have all the handouts and notes from a class, they don't have them kept in a way that will help them study. Some students will have all their hand-outs and assignments haphazardly stuffed into a single binder without a clue as to how to keep things neat. Often I've passed students by their lockers and get a glimpse of what can only be described as a vertical trash bin.

Try this: Clean out your backpack, binders, and locker. Toss away old materials that you don't need and organize the items that are still necessary for each of your classes. You may need to do this at the end of each academic week until you form the habit of keeping your materials neat at all times.

#8 Be Attentive in Class

"Choice of attention - to pay attention to this and
ignore that - is to the inner life what choice of action
is to the outer. In both cases, a man is responsible
for his choice and must accept the consequences,
whatever they may be."

W. H. Auden

With the rate of children diagnosed with ADHD sky-rocketing in this country it seems only fitting to include this as one of the hints for students to find success in school. While the numbers of children *truly* experiencing ADHD seem to be greatly overblown, the fact is many students do have difficultly staying focused on lessons in class.   The best students in school have learned to focus their attention in class and are able to pay attention to lessons. These students get more out of lessons and do better academically on both teacher generated tests and standardized testing.

Students who do not pay attention in class often miss assignments, lose interest, fall behind, and ultimately leave the classroom with less understanding because they were unable to focus on the lesson. These students will easily get frustrated and frequently lose interest in class activities because of their lack of understanding.

There are many factors that have contributed to the increases in students' inabilities to focus in class including lack of sleep, poor nutrition, and an increase in cell phone use.   Perhaps the greatest contributing factor that inhibits classroom focus is children are overstimulated. In this increasingly fast-paced society a great demand is placed on children to keep up. Several studies have shown that children who are exposed to fast paced TV and video games later have more difficulty staying focused in classroom settings. Unfortunately the trend of shows and games with more colors, better graphics and increases in action will undoubtedly continue.

Try this: For the next two weeks implement strategies that will help you stay focused in class. Get your sleep, ask to move to the front of the class, avoid foods and drinks that are high in sugars and caffeine, and avoid over stimulating graphic amusements.

#9 Do Work the Day You Get It

"Procrastination is one of the most common and deadliest of diseases and its toll on success and happiness is heavy."
Wayne Gretzky

I've discovered through the years that it's really important for me to write down tasks and appointments as soon as I think of them. All of us have a tendency to forget things, and young people in school have a lot of things on their minds. While students are in class they may perfectly understand the steps to an algebraic equation, yet given the passage of time they will often forget part of the process that gets them to the correct answers. Repeating a task soon after you learn how to do something is the best way to reinforce your memory, thus better insuring your success. Doing your school assignments while the information is fresh is one of the best ways to grasp and master new concepts.

Some of the best students in school are the ones who seldom get behind. These students take care of assignments and projects early and will often be the kids who stand out academically. They are prepared to handle the demands of school better than the average student because they have gotten in the habit of completing tasks quickly without allowing work to pile up on them. These are the same students who can handle unexpected stressors, such as sickness, that can lead to poor grades. These students have learned that doing work early is one of the keys to their success.

One of the worst things a student can do is put off doing work. Students who get in the habit of procrastinating ultimately turn in work of lower quality. Students who put off doing their assignments are often the same ones who struggle to understand concepts, do poorly on tests, and end up getting poor grades. These students fail to recognize that the timing of their work is directly connected to their success. Students who develop a habit of putting off their school work begin a disappointing trend that will be very difficult to break, and will often lead them towards shirking responsibilities at home and later at work.

Try this: For the next two weeks complete any assignment the day you get the work. Whether it's a math worksheet, pages to read in English, or a poster to complete for science class, do the work right away. Don't limit your ability to succeed by procrastinating.

#10 Edit Your Writing Assignments

"The first draft of anything is shit."
Ernest Hemingway

"So the writer who breeds more words than he
needs, is making a chore for the reader who reads."
Dr. Seuss

Once a student turns in an assignment they never want
to revisit it again. For most types of assignments this
practice is acceptable; however, with writing it is different. Good writing requires editing, and editing requires
patience and discipline. The best writing students are the
ones who take the time to review their papers and are willing to go through the process necessary to produce quality
written work. Good writers learn that through editing they
are able to eliminate many errors while better conveying
a more precise meaning to what they desire to express.

A good practice in writing is once you finish a draft
walk away from it and revisit it later. It is amazing the
number of errors and overall stylistic changes you will
discover given some time away from a particular draft of
writing. Good writers will also get the opinions of others who have the ability to look at a piece of writing with
fresh eyes and can offer the author a different perspective.

Often one of the main reasons that poor students don't
do well in school is because they are minimalists. They
do the least amount of work possible to get by. Getting
students who have adopted this lazy attitude to edit their

own writing assignments is like pulling teeth from a honey badger. One of the few things that seems to work is to have these students read aloud what they have written. No one wants to sound dumb. Often when these students hear themselves reading their own writing it helps to inspire them to make necessary changes to improve the quality of their work.

Try this: The next time you finish a writing assignment be sure to give it a second look. Read your paper aloud and see if you can hear anything that might need to be changed. You may want to have someone review it who can offer you some advice about possible stylistic and grammatical changes.

#11 No Excuses - No One Wants to Hear Them

"Ninety-nine percent of the failures come from people who have the habit of making excuses."
George Washington Carver

I'm not sure when a large group in our society decided they were entitled to things without earning them, but it seems I've noticed more of these types in the last few years. These students often think that they are going to pass with good grades without putting in the effort it takes to earn positive results. They are quick with excuses used to justify their position. Unfortunately for these students, most schools and businesses have little patience for people who adopt an excuse-based system of existence.

I am often amazed at the difficult issues students work hard to overcome. Students who are able to overcome economic, educational, and family hardships are truly inspiring to be around because despite the strikes against them they are still able to rise above their situations and find success. The best students, the most successful athletes, and the people you want to work with the most are the types of people who approach their tasks with the responsibilities of ownership. These people don't make excuses for failure; rather they find ways to overcome obstacles that lead them towards successes.

Perhaps the greatest disappointment teachers experience is seeing students perform below their abilities. As educators we see patterns in behaviors and we can often predict outcomes of students who consistently attempt to use excuses to explain their inadequacies in producing quality work. At some point it becomes painfully apparent that these students will experience many difficulties when they leave school and attempt to enter the harsh realities of becoming a responsible adult.

Try this: For the next week make no excuses for anything. Don't blame your lack of effort or level of success on anyone or anything. Take complete ownership of the results of your actions. Be responsible for your actions and avoid complaining about things you cannot control while taking action on things you have power over. Remember: No one likes to be around a whiner!

Section 3 - Hints that You Can Work On Outside of School

- Section introduction..48
1 Get your sleep 49
2 Get a job 51
3 Look and dress the part..53
4 Read as much as you can 55
5 Post your goals...57
6 Eat a healthy diet..59
7 Use short study session with rewards 61
8 Don't study things you already know 63
9 Set aside quiet time each day................................65
10 Study for tests 67
11 Do your homework 69
12 Complete your assignment & turn work in..........71

Hints You Can Work on Outside of School

It can be argued that the most important part of a student's school day begins at home. Many of the big academic issues that students have to face at school can be worked on away from school. While completing homework is important, there are many other aspects that happen at home that contributes to a student's academic successes and failures. Teachers rely on a strong base of support at home for their students to show progress in the classroom.

This section contains the hints that students can work on away from school. The best students have the ability to remain focused on their academic goals even while they are at home. These students are driven to better themselves by seeking ways they can improve their chances of academic success. These outside of school hints lay the foundation for a positive school day.

P.S. If a person has the ability to think then their education never ends.

#1 Get Your Sleep

"It is a common experience that a problem difficult at night is resolved in the morning after the committee of sleep has worked on it."
John Steinbeck

Perhaps there is not a single thing more important to a person's health than getting consistent sleep. It is our daily chance to wash our brains and invigorate ourselves for life's needs. A person who is able to get their sleep is more energetic, sharper, and happier. Nothing replenishes well-being more than sleep. Getting sleep is the foundation for a person's ability to function at their peak potential.

On the other hand, a person who has inconsistent sleep patterns is more irritable, less efficient and generally not much fun to be around. No doubt that stress, which is one of the most crippling of conditions, is increased with lack of sleep. A sleep deprived person will make more mistakes, have a poor attitude, and generally develop more health issues.

Often students tell me they have been up to two or three in the morning texting friends, watching TV, or playing video games. These are the same students who I have observed to be consistently behind in class, hard to get along with, and ultimately grow to dislike school. Who wouldn't develop resentment towards something they viewed as interrupting their sleep? Attempting to teach students who are consistently sleepy is the equivalent of trying to reason with a person who is intoxicated – not much fun for the teacher and hopeless for the student.

For many people sleep is difficult to obtain for a variety of reasons. Things that may help a person sleep are: consistent bed time, avoiding caffeine, sleeping in the dark, turning off your cell phone, getting plenty of exercise, and reading in bed.

Try this: For the next week attempt to get eight to nine hours of sleep each night. Log your sleep hours and monitor your academic performance. At the end of the week do a self-examination on your attentiveness in class and your overall academic performance. Sleep well!

#2 Get a Job

"The price of success is hard work, dedication to the job at hand, and the determination that whether we win or lose, we have applied the best of ourselves to the task at hand."
Vince Lombardi

There is a lot of speculation by many experts on the value of students who have jobs and whether it helps or hurts their academic performance. I feel it depends entirely on the situation. With that said, I believe that the benefits of having a part time job can greatly increase a student's overall abilities to be ready for life.

Perhaps the most important factor of an individual's success is to acquire the ability to interact well with all personality types. There may be no better avenue to be exposed to personal interaction more than the workplace. Students who work begin to develop the coping skills necessary for success in the working world, a place where they will spend the majority of the rest of their life. While the citadels of education teach students the theoretical aspects of learning, the workplace teaches the practical.

Some students who never learn the values of work develop an attitude of entitlement. These students can often be out of touch with the realities that working people face each day. While I have found teachers to be great nurturers, they often lack the straight forward, no nonsense approach that only a boss can supply. I cannot think of a working environment where there is extra credit or tasks are accepted late. Bosses don't coddle when they have a slacker working for them, they fire.

Students who have jobs begin to build a sense of self-worth that only being employed can give. The confidence gained, the value of earning one's own money, and lessons of time management all can come from having a job. Most students who acquire work learn responsibilities that their peers will sometimes never begin to appreciate until they are well out of college. Having a job helps to build perhaps the most important value of all, that of maturity.

Try this: Obtain a part time job and work for a month. At the end of that time do a self-assessment. Ask yourself, "How does it affect my time management? Am I working too many hours or too few? Are my grades better or worse? How does having this job affect my overall feelings?"

#3 Look and Dress the Part

"Look your best - who said love is blind?"
Mae West

For good or bad we are judged by how we look. While it may be short sighted to make generalizations about others based on how they look, it happens more often than not. Our outward appearance is how others perceive us and it is often how our reputations are gained or lost. Student who dress neatly and keep themselves well groomed gain more favor from their peers as well as adults. While this may not be right, it is a rule of nature to be attracted towards appearances that are pleasant to the eye. That is one of the keys to evolutionary success.

Students with poor attitude can often be spotted in the classroom by their appearance. While a child's economic issues may contribute to them looking unkempt, it is often a combination of the child not knowing or caring how to look decent for school and the parents not paying attention to what their child is wearing. This partly explains why some students will be waiting for the bus in freezing temperatures wearing shorts and a T-shirt, and others are dressed up as if they are attempting to attract late night customers. I've seen students rolling into school wearing pajamas and shuffling from class to class with slippers on. These same students are often behind in their work while at the same time being a clear distraction in the classroom.

We will often act how we appear. If a student is sloppy and out of order it is a good chance that same practice is seen in the student's work. Looking sharp doesn't equate to producing quality work, but it can enhance a student's respectability and put them in the right mindset to learn. With that said, I've seen some of the biggest slobs in the world be straight A students. While looking the part may not produce a 4.00 G.P.A. it does help to dress for success.

Try this: For the next week take extra time in preparing how you look for school. Dress neatly and make sure your clothes are clean and fit you properly. Pay attention that you are well groomed and your personal hygiene is in order. See if looking good and feeling confident about your appearance doesn't help you feel better and improve your overall academic performance.

#4 Read as Much as You Can

"I find television very educating. Every time somebody turns on the set, I go into the other room and read a book."

"Outside of a dog, a book is a man's best friend. Inside of a dog it's too dark to read."
Groucho Marx

Reading is perhaps the greatest activity a student can do that will increase their knowledge and overall understanding of the world. Nearly everything a student does that relates to academic success is related to and based on their ability to read. Almost every task in school is centered on reading. It is the core and at the foundation of academic success. As the old saying goes, the more you read the more you know.

Students who hate school are more often than not kids who are reading below grade level. Students who struggle with reading will ultimately experience frustration and anger. These students are at risk to achieve less in school and to develop animosities towards parents and teachers who attempt to get them to read. It is not much of an argument to see the correlation between reading levels and crime. It is no wonder then that, according to the National Institute for Literacy, **70% of prisoners fall into the lowest two levels of reading proficiency**.

I have found the number one reason students don't like to read is because they are below the reading level necessary for the book or text at hand. This makes perfect sense. Having a student read at levels well above their capabilities is like attempting higher levels of algebra and geometry while only possessing the rudimentary understanding of addition and subtraction. Trying to read material that is greatly above a student's ability will serve to reinforce a student's negative feeling towards reading and often towards learning in general.

Try this: For the next two days instead of watching TV, playing video games, or being involved in social media, try reading. Read anything from magazines, to books, to articles on the web. See how you feel after you replace your current visual stimulations with reading. Remember to read, read, and read some more!

#5 Post Your Goals

"Our goals can only be reached through a vehicle of a plan, in which we must fervently believe, and upon which we must vigorously act. There is no other route to success."
Pablo Picasso

The majority of successful people have goals for themselves. They may set their sights on a career they desire or a type of car they'd like to one day own. Some might set money aside for a vacation, while others have goals for physical fitness. The common thread of people who are successful is that they are goal oriented individuals who, through hard work, achieve the things they desire. Writing down your goals is one of the things that strong students do. By writing down your goals you focus your desires and set your sights on things you want to achieve. By physically putting your thoughts to paper and posting these goals you have in a way declared a commitment and challenge to yourself.

Unfortunately I have found one of the most difficult things to inspire is motivation. Students who lack the gumption to succeed are often the most difficult to be around because their laziness is a contagion. These students must be inspired to set goals that are easy to attain so they can start to build the foundation of experiencing successes. Long term goals may not work for these students. It is often best to concentrate on baby steps.

Your goals may look similar to something I have recently done for myself. The following are my goals for this book:

Goals for me:

1. Finish writing first draft of hint book by early-summer
2. Complete self-edit by mid-summer
3. Find a publisher by mid-fall
4. Share success with other educators

Try this: Make a list of 5 achievable academic goals you have for the current grading period. Be specific, i.e. "I will raise my grade in English by one letter." Once you have created your list post it in a place that you will see it every day. At the end of the grading period assess your success rate at achieving your goals and make a new list to post for the next grading period.

#6 Eat a Healthy Diet

"One should eat to live, not live to eat."
Benjamin Franklin

I had a student not long ago that would start each day in my class with a twenty ounce soda and a bag of chips. This turned out to be his typical breakfast during the entire semester. One day he walked in my first period class drinking from a two liter bottle of Mountain Dew. This child was obese, often fatigued, struggled academically, and had consistent discipline issues. He had obviously not learned that a healthy diet is one of the basic principles towards living a happy life.

Children who have food insecurities are more likely to suffer academically than students who are confident in knowing where their next meal is coming from. The majority of these students are living in poverty, and their lack of adequate nutrition is a byproduct of their **socio-economic** situation. These children come from families who have a hard time preparing healthy meals for their kids because of many factors that affect those struggling to make ends meet.

Food choices are one of the main contributions to a person's overall health. There have been recent studies in both Great Britain and Australia that link the consumption of fast food in children to lower IQ scores. It turns out that eating poorly not only makes you fat and causes health problems, but it also lowers your cognitive abilities.

Here are some sobering facts compiled by the Center for Disease Control and Prevention:
- Childhood obesity has more than doubled in chil-

dren and quadrupled in adolescents in the past 30 years.
- The percentage of children aged 6–11 years in the United States who were obese increased from 7% in 1980 to nearly 18% in 2012. Similarly, the percentage of adolescents aged 12–19 years who were obese increased from 5% to nearly 21% over the same period.
- In 2012, more than one third of children and adolescents were overweight or obese.

Try this: For the next week enjoy more fruits and vegetables. Avoid processed foods, sugars, and sodas. Make it a priority to not eat any fast food. After just one week assess how your feel. Eat healthy and be wise!

#7 Use Short Study Sessions With Rewards

"Before the reward there must be labor. You plant before you harvest. You sow in tears before you reap joy."

Ralph Ransom

I remember during my first year of college I had a classmate named Tom who always earned A's but never seemed to study. I recall him playing tennis just an hour before a midterm and thinking to myself that he must be very smart. Tom was smart - he was not gifted with extra intelligence - but he knew efficient ways to prepare for tests. As I later discovered, Tom would have intense study time lasting between 15-25 minutes, after which he would reward himself with a break. He would later tell me that by test time he knew everything. He would practice this method several times in the days leading up to big tests. He told me after each study session he would always reward himself with small things like a bite to eat, a TV show, or a game of tennis.

Studying in short intensive sessions is like hearing a song over and over again. After the first listen you may only remember an impression of the song. By the time you hear it a second time you're able to retain a little more. After several times of hearing the same song over a period of a few days most people know the entire song and can even sing along. This same method of retaining information is what Tom used to prepare for tests. By incorporating rewards at the end of each study session he was giving himself reinforcement for studying at the same time learning self-discipline that ultimately resulted in earning good grades.

Some students will try to pull an all-night study session before a big exam. While this method may work for a handful of students, it screams of desperation, and has about the same rate of success as throwing a 60 yard Hail Mary pass at the end of a football game. Trying to cram information in your head at the last minute just leads to a lot of frustration and usually does not produce good results.

Try this: Begin using this method right now for the next test you have. If you want to do something fun today make that your reward, but only after you have an intense but short study session. Do this several times the next few days and see how you will better retain the materials needed to score well on your test. Good Luck!

#8 Don't Study Things You Already Know

"I do not like to repeat successes; I like to go on to other things."
Walt Disney

No one likes to redo work, but it seems when it comes to studying most students like to review things they already know when preparing for tests. Perhaps the reason students study known material is the comfort of reviewing something that provides them with positive feedback creating a sense of success. The practice of reviewing known material is a waste of energy and it takes away from time that could be spent studying and learning information that is not yet known. Good students have learned to review things they are unclear about until they get to a point of understanding, then they move their focus towards more challenging and unknown information.

A good example of over studying is the use of flashcards. Say a student is preparing for an upcoming math test using 30 flashcards that the teacher had everyone make. At the beginning of the review process a particular student knows that $2 \times 5 = 10$, in fact this same student already has mastered ten of the flash cards, yet in preparing for the test he still reviews all 30 cards. This is redundant and a waste of the student's time. During the review process the known cards should be set aside and not studied. By doing this it gives the student more time to concentrate his focus on the cards he is still uncertain about.

Weak students desire the comfort of being correct, so

they don't take the chances of learning new things that test and challenge them. They are content with their previous knowledge and get stuck reviewing the same materials over and over again rather than attempting to acquire new information and new concepts of understanding. Many weaker students lack the drive and confidence to attempt to analyze and master ideas that are new and perceived as being difficult to comprehend.

Try this: For your next big test, only review the study materials that you are uncertain about. Once you have mastered the understanding of something don't continue to study those materials, rather focus your study time on things that you are still unsure of. Work smart. Don't waste your time reviewing things you know that you know.

#9 Set Aside Quiet Time Every Day

**"Dogs are wise. They crawl away into a quiet corner
and lick their wounds and do not rejoin the world
until they are whole once more."**

Agatha Christie

Our society is inundated with things to keep us oc-
cupied. School aged children as well as adults are bom-
barded with pacifiers that take the form of cell phones
and computers that connect us to a network of thousands
of sites competing for our attention. Rates of children
diagnosed with ADHD are at all-time highs, while the
demands on children to interact at accelerated paces have
put more pressure on students to succeed in academics, the
arts, and athletics. Perhaps the reason we have so many
children who have limited abilities to focus is because we
have conditioned them through excessive stimuli to be that
way. In a way we are being forced by the advances of
our technology to evolve faster than our abilities to cope
with the changes that are demanded.

Many of the best students have learned that one of the
keys toward developing a mind that has better reasoning
abilities is to give their brains a chance to reset through
deliberate times of inactive relaxation. Momentary
disengagement from the daily routine is one of the best
ways for students to develop better focusing skills. Good
students learn that daily quiet time away from the noisy
rush of typical activities can help them regroup their
thoughts and better focus their attention. It is no wonder

that companies have started to have exercise areas in their businesses. They have discovered they get more productivity out of their workers if they give their employees a positive chance to be away from tasks so they can clear their minds and be better able to refocus.

Weak students will seldom take the time to process difficult and complex problems. Thoughts that require steps are difficult for them to take because their thinking skills are often too busy multitasking and their minds have been trained to discover answers without reasoning through possible avenues of solutions. I've actually seen a student have his cell phone lying on his deck between him and the assignment he was working on. Between the appealing websites on a phone or the bland tasks of a worksheet it is no contest which one will capture a student's interest and attention.

Try this: Set aside at least 15 minutes each day to be alone and quiet. Give yourself a break from the busy schedule that so many of us have found ourselves in. Find a place away from external stimuli that is peaceful and give yourself some time to think or time to not think at all.

#10 Study for Tests

"I believed in studying just because I knew education was a privilege. It was the discipline of study, to get into the habit of doing something that you don't want to do."
Wynton Marsalis

Graduation is like paying a road toll. A few students can breeze through like having a driving pass on a day with zero traffic, while others are backed up in gridlock and looking on the floorboards for loose change. Basically put, a handful of kids can get to graduation with less effort because of their abilities while the majority must dedicate themselves to studying in order to achieve the grades necessary to be successful. Most students must put in the time studying for tests if they hope to do well.

Good students realize the importance of doing well in school so they make the efforts to prepare for tests. There are numerous strategies that work well for studying, and the most successful students learn what test preparation steps suit them. They take the time to do what it takes for them to do well.

A bad student can be the smartest kid in the building, but if they don't study for tests they more than likely will fail. Bright kids who fail due to lack of effort is perhaps a teacher's most frustrating experience. Luckily for teachers there are always less than gifted students who excel in school because of their strong work ethic. One of the ways students overachieve is by preparing for tests. They put in the time and dedication to studying.

Kids who struggle academically and don't prepare for

tests will most likely fail. If they choose not to study for tests, relying on homework and class work grades usually won't be enough to carry a student's scores to passing levels. It takes time and effort to prepare for tests, and students who don't study will find themselves one day looking for loose change to pay an expensive toll.

Try this: For the next two weeks dedicate yourself to studying. Prepare yourself for your classes by taking time each day to review class notes and teacher study guides. Read the assigned pages in the text and absorb the knowledge that is made available to you. See if your two weeks of dedication to study helps your grades and understanding of your subjects.

#11 Do Your Homework

"There's only one interview technique that matters... Do your homework so you can listen to the answers and react to them and ask follow-ups. Do your homework, prepare."
Jim Lehrer

I recently read a biography about Vince Lombardi, the legendary coach of the Green Bay Packers. Coach Lombardi was good at many things, but what I took from the book more than anything else was that he prepared his teams for their games. He studied game films, he practiced small things, and he knew the strengths and weaknesses of his opponents. Basically put, he did his homework and on game days his teams where ready. One of my favorite quotes from him is perhaps the shortest and in many ways the simplest, but it is powerful. He said, *"There is no substitute for work."*

Perhaps the most fundamental aspect of being a good student is completing your homework. Students who take the time to do work outside of class often come to realize the importance of their efforts - not just in raising their grades, but also in showing their dedication to hard work. The additional effort required to finish homework reinforces concepts covered in the classroom while increasing the students' knowledge and understanding of the subject.

One of the more predictable factors of students who fail is that they do not do their homework. Often this lack of effort is not entirely the fault of the student. Parents who don't encourage and make their children do homework are teaching them lessons about life that will lead to laziness, lack of drive, and a general dismissive outlook not only towards education but towards accountability in general. Parents dictate their children's schedules and the ones who don't guide their children towards getting work done at home should not be surprised when their kids bring home undesirable grades on their report cards and later in life end up living in the basement.

Try this: For the next two weeks complete all your homework assignments. Read the required pages, do all the math problems, and finish all your projects. Be the model student when it comes to doing homework. See if the work you do outside of class aids you in your understanding of what is going on during class.

#12 Complete Your Assignment & Turn Work In

"Focused, hard work is the real key to success. Keep your eyes on the goal, and just keep taking the next step towards completing it. If you aren't sure which way to do something, do it both ways and see which works better."
John Carmack

Some of the fundamental practices of being a good student is completing all your assignments and turning in your work. While this seems like a basic principle for students to follow, teachers will tell you that one of the main contributing factors to student failure is their lack of doing assignments. Good students turn in their work. I cannot think of a student that ever failed my class who turned in all their assignments. Turning in all your work is almost a guaranteed *'can't fail'* approach towards school. Teachers will also tell you that students who do all of their work are at the top of their classes.

Students who follow this hint might discover that their grades will go up because they are scoring points every time they turn in work. Compared to getting a zero on an assignment, a 50% grade is much better than no grade at all. While getting a 50% is still failing, it does supply students with points towards their overall grade, and hopefully some knowledge towards a future test which they can't acquire if they skip an assignment.

Unfortunately students who do poor in school seldom turn in their work. Failing grades will inevitably parallel work productivity. I've pleaded with students in the past to turn in their assignments, but some students refuse to do their work and these students fail school and don't graduate. I once ran into a student a few years after having him in class, who had failed out of school and never graduated. He was a nice young man, but he never did much in class even though he was more than capable of doing the work. He told me his number one regret in life was not staying in school and getting his high school diploma. He explained to me he always was having a hard time getting jobs because employers always looked to see if he had earned a high school diploma. He said he was going to try to get his GED. I wished him good luck, and as we parted I couldn't help but think if he had only taken the time to complete his work in school our conversation might have be happier.

Try this: For the next two weeks make sure to fully complete all your assignments and turn in all your work. Be diligent about not only completing your work, but also about turning in your assignments on time. See if this two week burst of getting all your work turned in makes a positive difference in your grades.

Section 4 - Hints that Require Internal Change

\- Section introduction..74

1 Never give up...75

2 Avoid drama...77

3 Get your exercise 79

4 Be passionate about your hobbies.......................81

5 Take pride in your work...83

6 Avoid multitasking...85

7 Look forward to changes 87

8 Have fun in school...89

9 he future is now...91

10 Discover your passions and follow them..............93

11 Take creative chances...95

12 Your grades - Your report card.............................97

Hints that Require Internal Changes

This section of hints may be the hardest set of skills to acquire because achieving personal changes depend greatly on the person's desire, drive, and attitude. Many things can be coached to a student but instilling gumption into an individual is such an intangible and subjective goal it becomes a most difficult attribute to gauge. This group of hints, if followed, can often be the most gratifying to accomplish because changes in one's core internal beliefs are often very difficult.

Kicking many undesirable habits require changes within. Friends, family, teachers, and others may help a person with many of these hints, but ultimately the individual must make the changes themselves. Unlike many of the hints that can easily be measured based off results, these goals require more of a self-assessment which can be difficult to evaluate. While it can be easy to notice changes in others, it is often hard to see changes in ourselves. This section could easily be titled *you're on your own,* because unlike other chapters the hints in this group require internal changes that can only occur through self-determination and can only be assessed by an honest review.

P.S. Remember the only person you truly can never lie to is you.

#1 Never Give Up

"I'm not saying it's going to be easy. Nothing in life is easy. But that's no reason to give up. You'll be surprised what you can accomplish if you set your mind to it. After all, you only have one life, so you should try to make the most of it."
Louis Sachar

"You just can't beat the person who never gives up."
Babe Ruth

Success has a tendency to drive people to want to acquire more. When we accomplish tasks our brains tell us, "Good job!" The brain rewards us by zapping us with dopamine that gives us a neurological boost that motivates us. This inspires us to repeat the experience that releases this chemical. It's like we have built in our brains a little drug dealer that rewards us when we accomplish things.

The failing student has a tendency to give up rather than attempt to complete something that is difficult or hard to understand. When assignments start to frustrate them or they see their progress as inadequate they will stop what they are doing and attempting to find satisfaction in other areas. Often these other avenues are not related to academic pursuits and can be detrimental to their success and that of others around them.

As a student it can be very tempting to throw in the towel when you realize you are failing or behind in a class or an assignment. Giving up is an easy way out of many situations that cause us anxiety. Walking away from a difficult problem may alleviate a person's immediate stress, but it is also habit forming. People who give up on school have a tendency to give up on work, and give up on others. Basically they give up on themselves. Too often people never begin to reach their potential because they gave up too soon or simply quit without really trying to see what they could achieve if they truly set their minds to something.

Try this: For the next week fully complete any activity you begin. See any assignment you begin through to its conclusion. This approach can easily apply to washing all the dishes as well as completing all academic assignments. At the end of the week assess your success rate and grade yourself on seeing things through. Don't give up!

#2 Avoid Drama

"I believe there should be no more drama, but it's everywhere you go. It's just about how you get out. You've gotta bob and weave because it's everywhere. How do I keep the drama low? It's about using your head."
                                        Mary J. Blige

At the beginning of each semester I always have my students list some academic and personal goals they want to achieve. I commonly get answers like, *"Get good grades,"* or *"Stay out of trouble."* I started to notice however that over the years several students would write, *"Stay away from drama."* This is something as an adult I discovered I had forgotten. Dealing with peers during the school years is often something many students really struggle with.

Top students in the building seem to never be overly concerned about issues that others are having. Not to say that these students are not empathetic, rather they just don't seem to dwell on the many issues that others surround themselves with. These students are able to stay focused on their agenda and goals while not getting caught up in the superficial exploits and dramas of their fellow students.

Social media has tapped into people's basic desire to be nosy. Unfortunately many minds are set to think about what others are saying and doing, while not being as concerned about taking care of their own responsibilities. It is no wonder that people spend a tremendous amount of time and energy looking into what other people are up to by checking out what is happening through their media sites. Our voyeuristic society that is magnified by social media has created situations where people depend on gossip, hearsay, and rumor to fuel their desire to be curious, but instead of filling people with knowledge it seems to leave them empty of anything that is substantial or important.

Try this: For the next two weeks avoid any type of gossip. Don't listen to it, don't play it forward, and don't create any. Avoid social media sites. Avoid trash magazines and website that talk about others. Take care of your own business and try not to be concerned about other people's affairs.

#3 Get Your Exercise

"The medical literature tells us that the most effective ways to reduce the risk of heart disease, cancer, stroke, diabetes, Alzheimer's, and many more problems are through healthy diet and exercise. Our bodies have evolved to move, yet we now use the energy in oil instead of muscles to do our work."
David Suzuki

While the freshman 15 may not be an accurate amount of weight gain seen by first year college students, it is common for many to experience some version of the fresher spread. One of the contributing factors to this weight gain is lack of exercise. As the amount of work load increases for college students their levels of stress rises. While exercise is a key factor that helps alleviate stress, it is often seen as too time consuming and is often ignored. People who exercise are better able to avoid illness and stress while looking and feeling better.

Our brains as well as our bodies need exercise. According to a study by The American College of Sports Medicine, on a 4.0 grade scale, students who exercised vigorously seven days a week had GPAs that were, on average, 0.4 points higher than those who didn't exercise. People who get exercise get better grades, ultimately leading them to get better jobs. One could easily argue that human evolution is advanced by those in the population who generationally participate in exercise.

Students who fail are generally less healthy than their peers. A recent study, published in the Journal Child Development, followed 6,250 children from kindergarten through fifth grade and discovered that those students who were obese throughout that period scored lower on math tests than non-obese students. These findings make total sense. Kids who are less healthy miss more days of school, thus causing them to be behind in receiving instruction that their more healthy peers are getting because they are in class.

Try this: For the next two weeks try to get at least 20 minutes of exercise every day. The intensity of your workout should vary on your level of fitness. See if your workout can be part of a lifestyle change. At the end two weeks do a self-evaluation of how incorporating exercise has made you feel.

#4 Be Passionate About Your Hobbies

"Today is life - the only life you are sure of. Make the most of today. Get interested in something. Shake yourself awake. Develop a hobby. Let the winds of enthusiasm sweep through you. Live today with gusto."

Dale Carnegie

It doesn't surprise me to see students who are involved in activities at school are the same ones who are consistently making honor roll each grading period. These students are the ones who enjoy school partly because they take part in what is happening. These students are interested and engage in opportunities that are available to them. They are in the band, they play sports, they are involved in clubs, and they participate in student government.

Many of the activities at school are a result of students developing passions for various hobbies. Hobbies help to build confidence levels by giving students a sense of personal achievement while strengthening self-esteem. Hobbies are, in a sense, a gateway to learning, and often a way of converting interest into future careers. Kids whose interests are sparked through hobbies get involved in the activities of life while exercising their minds and challenging their thinking skills.

Students who struggle with achieving success are often the ones that don't get involved in activities at school. These students have a tendency to shy away from attempting to broaden their knowledge while staying in their comfort zones. Students who don't get involved are in danger of watching life pass them by as a spectators rather than being participants. A passive activity, such as watching television, shuts the mind down. People who spend their time as spectators don't do, they just view. They have missed an essential point of life which, I feel, is learning through experiencing and exploring what the world has to offer.

Try this: Think about the things that spark your interest. Follow your passions. Get involved in activities that excite and challenge you. Be bold and shove shyness aside and learn to do the things you feel will make you the happiest. Take chances and try new things that may risk your comfort zone. Never stop exploring things that you want to find out more about.

#5 Take Pride in Your Work

"Disciplining yourself to do what you know is right and important, although difficult, is the highroad to pride, self-esteem, and personal satisfaction."

Margaret Thatcher

I once worked for a potter who if he wasn't satisfied with what he had created would destroy the piece. As he was breaking up some bowls he had thrown that had only the slightest flaws I asked him why he wouldn't just sell them at a discount. His answer, *"Because my name is on them."* He didn't have to explain anything else. He took pride in his art and he wasn't about to have his name associated with work that was not up to his standards.

Good students learn that taking pride in their assignments helps them to produce quality work, ultimately rewarding them with higher grades. The first grade student who receives a gold star sticker on an assignment feels the need to build on that success and will desire to get that positive stroke again from their teacher. As adults at work we take pride in receiving accolades from our peers and it produces a desire get positive feedback again. Success builds on success because receiving praise is addictive and it never gets old.

The student who turns in work and says, *"Good enough,"* may someday turn into the carpenter that realizes their work is sub-par but will still say, *"Well, I can't see it from my house."* This 'don't care' approach is a sign of having a poor attitude and it shows a complete lack of self-pride. Unfortunately this is a major characteristic of students who fail. Poor students often will adopt an attitude of not caring about academics to make failures become less painful and less important to them. This *"it doesn't matter if I don't care approach"* is a short term solution for dealing with their academic inadequacies, however it is habitual and it easily turns into an approach these students take with them for the rest of their lives.

Try this: For the next week turn in your best work. Give your best effort in all the work you turn in to your teachers. Expand this and give your best effort in doing any chores and giving a 100% at work. Take some pride what you produce, and remember, your work is a reflection of you.

#6 Avoid Multitasking

"Do three things well, not ten things badly."
David Segrove

"You can do two things at once, but you can't focus effectively on two things at once."
Gary Keller

I once pulled up next to a woman at a stop light who took multitasking to a whole new level. As we waited for the light to change I noticed her small dog that was sitting on her shoulder staring at me through the open window. The dog had what I can only suspect was a concerned look on his face. The lady was smoking a cigarette and talking on her cell phone. I could also hear her stereo blaring in the background. Needless to say, I was glad I was in the turning lane. She obviously had too many things going on at the same time and I'm afraid that paying attention to driving was not one of them.

Good students have the ability to focus their attention on individual tasks and problems without allowing themselves to get distracted by other forms of stimuli. These students remove distractors that will get in the way of their attentiveness. They turn off the music, they don't engage in conversation, and they ignore the many forms of social media that seems so engrossing to many of their peers. These students realize their full attention is required to get the most out of any task they wish to perform well on.

Poor students will unsuccessfully attempt to accomplish academic work while allowing other forms of stimuli to enter their senses, thus retarding their ability to focus fully on the task at hand. They will study with the TV on, attempt to do homework while eating, or be in class texting a friend while the teacher is explaining a concept. These students attempt to juggle too many items at once and are bound to drop some of the more important things. Our fast paced and ever advancing technological society is intriguing. Unfortunately, the upsurge in attractive and alternative forms of entertainment seems to be creating generations that are losing their ability to concentrate.

Try this: For next week monitor the number of times you catch yourself multitasking at school or when you are doing homework. Attempt to focus on one thing at a time. Try not to allow distractions when you are concentrating.

#7 Look Forward to Changes

"Change is invigorating! If you don't accept new challenges, you become complacent and lazy! Your life atrophies! New experiences lead to new questions and new solutions! Change forces us to experiment and adapt! That's how we learn and grow!
Bill Watterson

I remember being very worried about going into third grade math. Third grade was the year we switched from the easy books that you just wrote your answers in, to using our own paper to write out problems. Granted, this wasn't a big change, but one that I wasn't looking forward to. Shifts in school will happen all the time and students who have the ability to be flexible are more able to cope with changes when they occur. The best students recognize that change is a part of growth and they look forward to the challenges and novelties of adjustments to their learning. In short, they see change as an opportunity not as a hassle.

Adaptability is a key ingredient to success in the work place. Employers today are looking for people who have the skill sets which allow them to be accommodating with the diversities of a growing and competitive economy. Employers do not hold much value in their workers if they don't have the ability to evolve with changes that are necessary for growth and development. Many employees find themselves forced into retirement or fired -- not because of their age, but because of their lack of willingness to try new things and to change with innovations within their business.

Some students cannot cope if you attempt to change something from their daily routine. These students want to stay in their comfort zone. Students constantly look for patterns to follow, so when patterns are broken many students will have difficulty adjusting to new changes. Not having the ability to change and grow shows stagnations in thought and an unwillingness to evolve and adapt.

Try this: Next time you experience a major change in school think of it as an opportunity rather than a hassle you have to deal with. Always be ready for change because it happens often. Embrace changes because being able to adapt in different situations is one of the keys to personal growth.

#8 Have Fun in School

"I never did a day's work in my life. It was all fun."
Thomas Edison

"People rarely succeed unless they have fun in what they are doing."
Dale Carnegie

Thinking back to my days as a student, I remember the classes I learned the most in were the ones that were the most fun. In many cases if a student has fun in class they will learn more of the content area and achieve better grades. Humor works as a way to learn. A growing body of research suggests that the effective use of comedy in the classroom can improve performance by reducing anxiety, while increasing participation and motivation to concentrate on material.

Good students typically see school as a fun place and they realize that being in school is perhaps the only time in their lives that they'll be among the greatest concentration of their peers. They enjoy the camaraderie that the school environment creates, and they look forward to the fun that classes bring. Students who possess a positive attitude are more open to learning.

Poor students may also have fun at school, but often at the expense of other students, teachers, and ultimately themselves. They cannot equate fun with learning and they think their forms of fun are more important than the overall task at hand of learning. Class clowns are only funny if their humor does not take away from the learning. Often the funny kids can be steered towards becoming true leaders in the classroom while helping to make the learning environment more enjoyable for everyone. Occasionally, however, a student will sabotage a class with their antics.

Often poor students don't have much fun in school. There are many factors that contribute to this: depression, lack of participation, poor health, inadequate placements, or an overall negative attitude towards school. Whatever the reasons, their lack of enjoyment negatively affects their learning abilities and that of anyone around them.

Try this: For the next week look for things in class that make you smile. Maybe it's the goofy kid that sits next to you or a funny thing a teacher always seems to do. Involve yourself in team projects and study groups with people who are serious about learning and can have fun at the same time.

#9 The Future is Now

**"Each of us has been put on earth with the ability
to do something well. We cheat ourselves and the
world if we don't use that ability as best we can."**
George Allen

Back in the 1970s the Washington Redskins had a
head coach by the name of George Allen who is often
credited with the saying, *"The future is now."* His teams
were comprised mainly of older players, many of whom
had been dismissed by other teams in the league. In fact,
they were lovingly called the *over the hill gang* because
of their ages. Coach Allen's message to these veterans
was that they basically didn't have any time to wait if they
wanted to be a winning team. There probably was no
such thing as a *rebuilding year* in Coach Allen's mindset.
I'm sure that the carpe diem philosophy was something
that George Allen practiced and instilled in his players
wherever he coached.

Good students come to understand that their time is
now. They don't push things off until later or pine for a
distant future when everything will be alright. They take
charge of the time they have now because they realize
that this is their moment to shine. They don't waste time,
rather they use what time they have to do things they enjoy
and that will help them have a wide and meaningful life.
These students don't let tragedies get the best of them;
they learn from life's misfortunes and turn these experiences into ways to help them grow as a person. In short,
these students embrace life and enjoy it.

Perhaps the greatest injustice a person can do themselves is to exist in a life unlived. It is sad, but true, that many students just go through the motions of education without experiencing the many wonderful things that school offers. These students miss out on so many interesting and joyful things that are free and only available while they're in school. Many times these students eventually wake up and start to discover the numerous things they've missed. It is never too late to begin to live your life.

Try this: Adopt the future is now mentality. Realize that your time here is limited and that your chances to improve yourself start today. Limit the time that you waste on things that don't help you grow as a person. Remember that life is our greatest gift, that's why they call it the present.

#10 Discover Your Passions and Follow Them

"Passion is one great force that unleashes creativity, because if you're passionate about something, then you're more willing to take risks."
Yo-Yo Ma

One of my favorite places to see is a workshop of an artist. Next to being creative myself, seeing a person who is working in their element is perhaps my greatest pleasure. Entering the working area of someone who has honed a skill is one of the most uplifting spaces a person can be around. Can you imagine what it must have been like to walk into Picasso's studio or to see Thomas Edison tinkering in his workshop? What would it have been like seeing the Beatles working out a song in a recording session? When you are following your passions and doing something special the creative atmosphere around you is electric and very contagious.

Students who are able to discover and follow their passions are more creative and driven to perform well because they are doing things that interest them. It only makes sense that the subjects students enjoy will be the ones they typically excel in. When students reach college and are able to take classes in their major they will thrive in these subjects because they are surrounded by topics that are in line with things they feel passionate about. People who follow their academic passions are typically happier than those whose pursuits are based on financial gains.

It seems that weaker students often lack direction and interest in many of the things that life has to offer. These students seldom have the structured support that helps them get involved in school and community activities that so often serve as a spark that potentially can begin their interest in things that inspire them to learn and do more with their lives. Most kids start school pretty fired up about learning and discovering, however some students will lose this passion as they experience academic and social failures. The more a student fails the less likely they are to take risks to follow their passions - both academically and personally.

Try this: To discover your passions, experiment. If you want to find out about something that intrigues you, take some steps towards following what it is you are interested in. Make discoveries of things that inspire you, and then follow these passions. Live for the things you enjoy and don't become tied to doing things that don't lead to your happiness.

#11 Take Creative Chances

"Take a chance! All life is a chance. The man who goes farthest is generally the one who is willing to do and dare."

Dale Carnegie

What is it that compels students to attempt academic risks in the classroom? Why are some pupils willing to go first, quick to raise their hands, or volunteer to come to the board while others will never push themselves toward taking academic chances? These risk taking students seem to have confidence in attempting new tasks despite the chance of even being wrong. Typically classroom interaction is tied directly to previous results. Students who take more creative chances are the ones who have received positive feedback from attempting risks in the past, while those students who have experienced previous failures and negative feedback are less likely to attempt any future chances in the classroom.

Fear of failure keeps many students from taking risks. Often educators will notice students participate less at secondary levels where the demand for work and level of difficultly increases. It is often very difficult for students who struggle in school to take academic risks. They have become so shy and hurt by early failures that stepping out on a limb is too risky for them to consider. Think about the student who is afraid to read aloud in class because of the possibility of not knowing a word and feeling inadequate when making a mistake. This student will likely not want to volunteer to read in class due to their fear of being per-ceived as sounding dumb. Unfortunately, many students who experience failure in the classroom will seek to find positive feedback from other, more destructive influences.

Students who take creative chances are the ones who challenge themselves not only in the classroom but in other avenues of life. These creative risk takers will ultimately be the ones who will reap the rewards of trying new things while evolving into the movers and shakers of our future.

Try this: Take a creative chance academically this semester. Step outside of your comfort zone. Join a club at school that challenges you. Be bold and take an elective that sounds interesting. Do something different and get out of any rut you may have started to dig.

#12 Your Grades - Your Report Card

"What I always say is, 'Do every job you're in like you're going to do it for the rest of your life, and demonstrate that ownership of it."
Mary Barra

Two boys meet in the hallway after report cards have been given out. One student looks at his grades and says, *"I got an A in English!"* The other student in dismay says, *"She gave me an F!"* In this example one student owns his grade, while the other student attempts to disassociate from his poor scores by saying the grade is what the teacher decided to give him. In both cases their grades were earned, but the second student doesn't want to assume ownership of a bad grade, so he claims it was something the teacher gave to him instead of owning the poor grade he actually achieved. Of course, not many students will fess up and admit that they earned a poor grade. I don't think I ever heard a student say, *"I earned an F!"*

Good students take a vested interest in their grades because they realize their scores are an extension of who they are. They know that earning good grades will ultimately help them have a better chance at being more successful in life. They realize that they have the biggest stake in their future, and they work hard to achieve higher grades because it will provide them with more opportunities for advancement. They understand ownership and they take their responsibilities seriously because they know it will help them in the long run.

Poor students often refuse to own their negative issues. I had a student complain about how his desk is too small because he constantly is knocking his materials to the floor. He fails to recognize that other students in class have the same type of desks but they don't seem to have any issues. He blames the desk as oppose to accepting the responsibility himself. Students who have conflict personalities issues will often struggle with this goal. These students are unable to accept their own shortcomings because they are preoccupied with blaming any of their own failures on something outside of themselves

Try this: Assume ownership of the grades you earn. Have a vested interest in the scores you achieve because they are a direct reflection of your abilities. Don't blame others for your failures or have excuses for your lack of success. Your report card is yours and no one else's. Own it!

Section 5 - Hints that May Require Some Help from Others

- Section introduction 100
1 Seek adult help 101
2 Avoid drugs 103
3 See teacher ASAP for makeup work 105
4 Find a mentor to talk to about grades 107
5 Get a study buddy 109
6 Get tutoring help 111
7 Attend review sessions for standardized tests 113
8 Hang out with smart people 115
9 Imitate positive role models 117

Hints that May Require Some Help from Others

One thing I've noticed about young people during the course of my teaching career is that they often have a difficult time asking for help. Perhaps they are shy and a bit intimidated. Some students are distrustful. Others hate to ask questions because they don't want to appear to be stupid. Whatever the case may be, many students have a hard time asking for help when they need it. Often students would rather take a lower grade than seek the help that they know could improve their score. Learning to ask for and take good advice is one of the keys to becoming a better student and a more mature individual.

The hints in this section require students to step outside of their comfort zone by seeking help from others. Teachers, parents, coaches, and administrators are just some of the people students can turn to for advice and assistance. Students can empower themselves by becoming a strong self-advocate. Gaining knowledge is not difficult. Albert Einstein said, *"Intelligence is not the ability to store information, but to know where to find it."* We all depend on each other to gain strength and to become more self-aware.

P.S. Remember you are not alone. Lots of people are available to help. You just need to ask.

#1 Seek Adult Help

"Alone we can do so little; together we can do so much."
Helen Keller

One of the more difficult things for humans to do is to seek the advice of others. Humans are headstrong types of animals and we like to do what we want.   It is often quite hard for us to be open to input or seek the advice of other people. Students who excel at school are usually the ones willing to be advised and are wise enough to follow good counsel.

Often failing students are unwilling to listen to the advice of their parents and teachers. Many times failing students follow their own agendas and are uninterested in the possibilities of growth that comes with the challenges of changes. Many students who struggle in school lack the interpersonal relationships with adults who might be available to help. This often starts at home. It is only natural for a student to stay away from mature guidance if their own adult role models are lacking in abilities to provide a stable and growth oriented environment.

Growing up in today's society is one of the most difficult things for a person to have to go through. Young people face more superfluous external input then any time in history. It can be very confusing for many students to recognize what the best direction for them to set their goals towards and how to prioritize their actions for achievement.

Try this: The next time you have a question about the right thing to do ask the advice of three people you admire and who you think will give you the best advice. Consider what these three have to say and then act on the good advice you may have generated from their input.

#2 Avoid Drugs

"Drugs are a waste of time. They destroy your memory and your self-respect and everything that goes along with your self-esteem. They're no good at all."

Kurt Cobain

This may sound like one of the oldest bits of advice a person could give, but I would be remiss to leave it out of this book because it is so important towards the success of a young person's academic pursuits. Students who avoid drugs get better grades, have a higher self-esteem, and are generally happier people. People whose cognitive abilities have not be compromised by drug use achieve more and are physically and mental more superior.

While drug use is no good at any age it is particularly crippling for young people whose minds are still developing. People who start taking drugs at an early age are likely to develop an abundance of negative health issues including depression, mental impairments, physical ailments, and addictive dependencies. According to the National Institute on Drug Abuse there are more deaths, illness, and disabilities from substance abuse than from any other preventable health condition. Today, one in four deaths is attributable to alcohol, tobacco, and illicit drug use. Prisons in this country are overcrowded with the majority of inmates finding themselves there on narcotic related sentences.

Drug use is far from limited to illegal use in this country. According to statistics from the Centers for Disease Control and Prevention, the United States represents 5%

of the world's population, yet 75% of prescription drug use. More teens die from prescription drugs than heroin/ cocaine combined. It can be very difficult to avoid drugs considering the legal drug culture that our society is inundated with. It is little wonder that we live in a society that is overdosed when TV commercials are filled with ads for prescription and nonprescription drugs. While pharmaceutical and insurance companies enjoy profits, our healthcare costs spiral out of control and our children become more drug dependent then any of the previous generations.

Try this: Kids talk. Most kids have a pretty good idea who the drug users are in their schools. Observe your fellow students. How often are these students at school? What kinds of grades are these students earning? Ask yourself if you want to achieve their same level of academic success. Is it worth it?

#3 See Teacher ASAP for Missing Work

"If you could kick the person in the pants responsible for most of your trouble, you wouldn't sit for
a month."

Theodore Roosevelt

Students who excel in school plan ahead and are
responsible. They realize that when they miss a class
they are missing information that directly affects their
understanding of the material and their grade. It is not
surprising to see the correlation between good class attendance and high grades. Students who miss school fall
behind their peers socially, academically, and physically.
Perhaps the worst thing about missing school is the gap
it creates in the student's understanding of information
they might have obtained if they had been in attendance.
Students who are facing academic problems often have
or have had attendance issues.

The best students understand their responsibilities and
they take actions to get and complete any assignments
they missed due to being out of class. These students
understand that their academic successes and failures are
owned by them and they are willing to see to it that they
get information they missed on days they are out of school.
Most students who excel at school are seldom absent. It is
no surprise that students who are on honor rolls are often
the same kids who have very good attendance records.
They realize that one of the most important keys to success is being present.

Student who fail never seem to make up work they missed on the days they were out. I've been amazed at the number of times students will come to class after being absent for days and they never even inquire about what work they have missed. They often falsely assume that because they were gone it excuses them from any assignments they may have missed during their absence. This lack of basic understanding of responsibility is at the core of why many students fail. As a teacher I am constantly reminded of the fact that teaching accountability is one of my most important duties to my students.

Try this: *If you miss a day of school make a point of seeing the teacher the morning you return to get any information you missed. If you know you are going to miss a class tell the instructor in advance and see if you can get the work before your absence.*

#4 Find a Mentor to Talk to About Grades

"No matter what color you are, if you mentor some little boy or girl, you make a huge difference in their lives because they then model behavior that leads to success versus modeling behavior that doesn't."
Mario Van Peebles

If you ask teachers why they got into the profession of education they will often tell you that they were influenced by one of their former teachers, coaches, or administrators. It seems that most teachers remember the feeling they got from past educators who helped to inspire their academic goals and focus on their individual pursuits.

Many students who experience success in school view faculty members as people who can and will help them succeed. They realize that doing well in school is a springboard for their future and that teachers have the knowledge to help them achieve their goals. Good students don't isolate themselves from help; they have learned to take advantage of accepting good advice. They realize that the smartest students are not necessarily the ones gifted with great abilities, but the ones that know how to seek out help and act on good counsel. Seeking mentoring advice becomes very important when students are transitioning from high school to college levels because of the variety of demands individual schools will require.

It is hard to believe but some students actually view faculty members as enemies. It may be that these children never found success in school and at some point gave up and turned their lack of success into rejecting anything a teacher has to say. Some students are just shy and don't desire to interact with adults. Whatever the case may be, students who attempt to get through school without getting advice about academics are bound to make some mistakes that could have been easily avoided with some simple guidance.

Try this: Consider the adults who you have good relationships with at your school. Pick one or two of these people to talk with about your grades. Be honest with them about your academic goals and concerns. Be sure to ask questions about ways you can be more successful.

#5 Get a Study Buddy

"It seems to me that trying to live without friends is like milking a bear to get cream for your morning coffee. It is a whole lot of trouble, and then not worth much after you get it."

Zora Neale Hurston

During my earlier years of teaching I had two girls in one of my English classes that were best of friends and would work together on assignments. They helped each other prepare for tests and they worked on homework and projects together. If one of the girls was absent from class the other would collect any materials her friend would need. They had each other's backs. Both students earned A's in the course while at same time teaching me the valuable lesson of the buddy system approach towards learning and excelling.

By using the buddy system you develop a positive codependency where each person drives the other to perform well. This system helps each student become more accountable to the other because each learns to depend on the others' equal input for their mutual successes. While this approach may not always work due to an imbalance in work load, it does seem to produce positive results in work being turned in by both students involved. Perhaps the best outcome of this approach is that it teaches teamwork, which is a needed quality students must have when they eventually enter the work world.

Over the years I've noticed that most of the students who fail are those that are loners in class. Students who have true friends have a tendency to get pulled back up when they get behind in classes or have difficulties with understanding lessons. When a kid is having trouble in class their friends will help them. Those students who are loners often do not have the network of friends that are available to help them succeed. There is a great deal of truth to the old saying: two brains are better than one.

Try this: For each of your classes seek out a person who you like and who you can depend on to complete assignments together and prepare for tests with. Remember: Being a study buddy is a two way street.

#6 Get Tutoring Help

"The man who can make hard things easy is the educator."
Ralph Waldo Emerson

I remember my junior year in high school as being the hardest. That year I was getting behind in chemistry and was starting to feel very lost in class discussions. Eventually I sought help from a student in class named Randy who seemed to know what he was doing. After school I would bug him to help me with homework assignments. He would do problems for me which allowed me to see the steps needed to get the right answers. I'm sure this helped me pass the class, but more importantly it taught me to seek assistance when I was struggling to understand something.

Smart students may not always have the answers but they pursue ways to discover and understand solutions to questions. They seek knowledge rather than right answers. These students have learned to put their egos aside and seek advice when they are faced with information they don't understand because they realize the importance and need for understanding.

Often weak students want to get answers right but they are not always concerned about understanding solutions. They are unwilling to take the extra step of getting tutoring to help them through lessons they are having trouble with. Teachers will tell you that tutoring reviews for standardized tests are filled with students who are not just attempting to pass but are trying to achieve higher scores. Unfortunately, teachers also know that the students who really need to be at these sessions seldom show up.

Try this: If you are having trouble in a class seek direct instructional help. Get a tutor to help you better understand what you may not be getting in class. Take care to get a tutor sooner than later. Don't hesitate in seeking help on lessons you are having trouble understanding.

#7 Attend Review Sessions for Standardized Tests

"They're testing us all the time."
Former Student

I have to say that the trend in this country to constantly have students jump through the hoops of standardized testing is perhaps the most ludicrous part of our education system. With that being said, standardized tests are the current hurdles. For students to move forward in their educational pursuits they need to do well on these types of assessments. While more classroom time is dedicated each year towards teaching to these types of tests, students often need extra help to be successful. It is becoming a regular practice that school systems are offering extra test review sessions before or after school hours to help students prepare. Students who attend these sessions will typically increase their test scores.

Many times teachers will provide credit incentives to encourage participation in their review sessions. Students who desire to increase their test and class scores will take advantage of these review opportunities. They will discover that they not only do better on the tests, but they improve their course grades as well. Teachers will attest that these review sessions are often missing the students they were designed to help. Students who struggle often view these types of tests as something not to be taken seriously, and they will fail to take the extra step of attending a review session that could help them achieve higher scores and better grades.

While states differ on the number and types of tests they require their students to take, all states test to a varying degree, and most colleges demand some form of entrance test as part of their administration policy. Student testing has become a multimillion dollar industry and school systems are forced to comply with the laws set forth by legislative policies. Some could argue that standardized testing has had the greatest impact in the last twenty years on how we educate our children. *Does it work? Is it worth it?* These are questions that states must address if they have the best interests of their children in mind.

Try this: Go to any extra review sessions teachers are offering to help you boost your scores on state or national tests. These review sessions will really help you do better on the tests and may help to boost your grades in the class as well. Two birds, one stone!

#8 Hang Out With Smart People

"Whatever you do in life, surround yourself with smart people who'll argue with you."
John Wooden

Several years ago at a high school where I was teaching a group of students did something I thought was unique and very wise. For the student council elections they ran as a group. They basically created a ticket and swept the school elections that year. These were bright students who figured out that as a group they could present themselves to the school in this novel way. As a team of smart kids they were able to feed off each other's ideas to create a campaign strategy that was appealing and successful.

Many like-minded students will be in the same classes because of placements based on tracking systems that schools still use. This practice, very early on, starts to divide students into academic and social groups. These students will have the same classes, share the same lunch times, and have many of the same friends because of the time they spend together. Because of their academic placements, students who do well in school end up being around their peers who are also doing well. These students have a tendency to get involved in common extracurricular school activities which is another trait of students who succeed.

Unfortunately students who are struggling are often placed in classes with peers who are at their same academic achievement levels. It is very difficult for a child to move out of these tracked ability levels by the time they reach secondary school unless parents are advocating for their placement change. Students who find themselves in certain groups can often have a difficult time finding friends who inspire and encourage them to better themselves. This can be one of the hardest hints to follow for young people because making changes in your peer groups is not easy. It only makes sense that students have a tendency to be drawn towards the kids they are most familiar with. Hopefully, those friends are the kind that can have a positive influence.

Try this: *Take a long hard look at the people you hang out with. Ask yourself if these are the people who you truly desire to be associated with. Start to build relationships with quality people who are smart and can challenge you to become a more thoughtful person.*

#9 Imitate Positive Role Models

"Typically, when you look for role models, you want someone who has your interests and came from the same background. Well, look how restricting that is. What people should do is take role models a la carte. If there's someone whose character you appreciated, you respect that trait."
Neal deGrasse Tyson

Most of today's music is generated not from original ideas but from variations of what musicians have done in the past. Very little of what is new is really new, rather a new version of what existed before. Much of our creativity can be attributed to the experience of what we are exposed to. One of the reasons students are assigned lessons about famous people is because these historical individuals often serve as good role models for young people.

Most students learn how to be a good person through the positive influences of their family. This is at the core of a person's ability to distinguish between good and bad behaviors. In many ways children are like parrots who repeat things they are exposed to. We model the behaviors of the people we are closest to. Children who are exposed to role models who are caring and nurturing will learn these skills much better than those who attempt to obtain these character traits through books and self-improvement classes.

Many times as educators we observe that our struggling students are those who are lacking proper role models who can teach them the skills necessary to do well in school. This can be a failure in the home, community, or the school itself. Regardless of where the shortcomings exist, students who lack adequate role models will seldom learn to be good students, and they often struggle to become good citizens in our society.

Try this: Pick three people you admire and write down the traits that you see in these people that you wish to emulate. Under these good qualities list the things you need to do in your life to reach these goals. It might look something like this:

Honesty	Dedication to a craft	Positive outlook
* Always tell the truth	* Practice more each week	* Get my sleep
* Never cheat	* Take extra lessons	* Good attitude

Section 6 - Hints that May Take a While

\- Section introduction...120
1 Avoid bad students 121
2 Maintain a positive attitude...............................123
3 Care about your G.P.A. 125
4 Be honest and have integrity.............................127
5 When you get down - get busy..........................129
6 Take a fun class each semester.........................131
7 Never sell yourself short 133
8 Don't beat yourself up when you fail.................135
9 Attack your weaknesses 137
10 Think of school as an opportunity to learn 139
11 Be your own hero – No one else will.................141

Hints That May take a While

One quality that I've noticed many of my students struggle with is patience. This is not surprising given the world we live in that provides us with so much instant gratification. It would be nice if positive personal changes could happen quickly, but many of the most profound shifts in a person's life don't happen overnight. Some students may struggle with the hints in this section if they expect to see results right away. These hints deal with changes that may take a student a long while to learn and implement in their daily routines. While you will experience some success while working on these hints don't be surprised if setbacks occur. These are longer term practices that may require periodic recommitments and reassessments to ensure that they are being continued. Keep your eyes on your goals and continue to strive for them using these hints successfully.

P.S.,

"Patience and perseverance have a magical effect before which difficulties disappear and obstacles vanish."

John Quincy Adams

#1 Avoid Bad Students

**"Associate with men of good quality if you esteem
your own reputation; for it is better to be alone than
in bad company."**
George Washington

Being around bad students can suck the life out of
a person. Failing students are often demeaning to be
around because they can discredit your imagination while
diminishing your abilities. A bad student is like a large
emotional sponge which absorbs all the good from the
people they come in contact with. The positive influences
from parents and teachers have a difficult time balancing
the impact of a student's negative social circle.

Often bad students can be funny and interesting.
Failing students frequently surround themselves with
some sort of drama that can be distracting from the daily
necessities of being a functional student. While this can
be an interesting distraction from the daily grind, it is also
something that people let themselves easily get sucked
into. It is no wonder that TV is filled with meaningless
stories of people in our society being completely foolish.
While this attraction to the lower common denominator
may be shocking and help to boost ratings, it's a complete
waste of time.

The good news is you have a choice of who you associate with. You can pick people to be around who are smart
and ultimately have a lot to offer you. It is hard to grow
as a person if the people you are around are not willing
or able to evolve. People will imitate the habits of those
around them. Making friends with smart people is one

of the best things you can do for yourself because it gives you an opportunity to learn from their positive attributes.

A bad student is like a drowning man; if you get too close they will pull you down with them. We become, more often than not, what the people around us are like. It is no wonder that the kids who flunk out of school always have plenty of friends with them. This becomes their social group outside of school and, unfortunately for a few, their peer group when they become incarcerated.

Try this: For the next week try to avoid any bad students you know. Don't get sucked into any of their concerns. Avoid these students in class, at lunch, and in the hallway. Let them find other suckers to feed off of. Your self-preservation is more important. At the same time try to seek others who can help you grow as a person.

#2 Maintain a Positive Attitude

"Nothing can stop the man with the right mental attitude from achieving his goal; nothing on earth can help the man with the wrong mental attitude."
Thomas Jefferson

There are not too many things that are as important to a person's growth and happiness as having the right attitude. Developing a good attitude is wonderful thing to have in school but it is one of the best tools to acquire for life. Students with a "can do" attitude are the leaders in school and more times than not become leaders at work and in the community.

Students with poor attitudes will have problems getting along with their parents, teachers, and peers. Often poor attitudes at school will later evolve into poor attitudes at work. Nothing makes a task more difficult than dealing with people who are hard to get along with. People who are haters have a dark cloud above them that covers anyone they get close to.

Strengthening ones attitude requires a desire to be a better person. The basic ways to begin to improve one's attitude is getting the right amount of sleep, eating well, and exercising. These practices set the ground work for a healthy body and mind. Once these are in place students can learn to foster a better attitude through several actions. The following are some important things to keep in mind when developing a positive attitude:

1. **Have purpose in your actions**. Think before you

act and ask yourself, *"Will the action I'm about to take be helpful or harmful to achieving my goals."*

2. **Avoid haters and find people with positive attitudes to be around.** Good vibes can rub off on you, so put yourself around people who are positive.

3. **Adopt an attitude of gratitude.** Simply put, work on being the most polite person you can be. It is amazing how a simple smile and a *thank you* is contagious.

Try this: Get a note card and track each time you catch yourself being negative about anything in school. This can apply to classes, teachers, friends, and overall feelings. At the end of one week look at your list and assess the reasons why you had these feelings. Ask yourself, "Do these feelings linger? Was I just being too negative?" Try to get a grip on why you felt the way you did and see if you can come up with ways to convert this negative energy into a positive attitude.

#3 Care About Your GPA

I have discovered that students who care about their grade point average, GPA, are the same students who consistently perform better in class. Students who have an awareness of their academic performance and level are more likely to focus on bringing their scores up than the students who are completely unaware of their grades. It has always confounded me that some students don't see their grades as an extension of themselves. Your GPA is a direct reflection of your academic achievement level, and one of the main factors that college admissions consider while deciding who gets to go to their schools.

To calculate your GPA use the following example:

Wendell's grades	Grade Values
Science - F	A = 4
Math - D	B = 3
English - A	C = 2
History - C	D = 1
Health/PE - B	F = 0
Graphic Art - A	Spanish - C

Wendell's grade value adds up to 16. Divide his grade value by the number of classes he is taking. $(16 \div 7 =$

2.29) So, 2.29 is Wendell's GPA. If Wendell were to bring his science grade up to an A his grade value would then add up to 20. (20 ÷ 7 = 2.86) So, 2.86 is Wendell's new GPA.

Try this: Calculate your current GPA. Are you an A, B, or C student? See if by the end of this grading period you can raise your GPA up. Set a goal and do it!

#4 Be Honest and Have Integrity

"Honesty and integrity are absolutely essential for success in life - all areas of life. The really good news is that anyone can develop both honesty and integrity."

Zig Ziglar

This sounds like a good piece of advice a parent might give to their child about how to live their life, but beyond that it is a positive habit for students to learn as well. Good students are honest with themselves. If students are honest with themselves they know when they have given their best effort on assignments and they admit it when they haven't. Successful students learn that being honest starts with themselves and it doesn't include excuses and justifications. Most teachers and parents know if you are working up to your potential so using excuses to avoid work just makes you seem lame in their eyes. Good students realize this and thus work hard to prove to themselves they are worthy of positive grades and praise.

Failing students have gotten into the bad habit of accepting excuses for themselves and often developing a false sense of justification for their actions. I had a student recently who was consistently showing up late to my class. His reasoning was that the lunch room was too far away from the classroom. In his mind he created a belief that it was OK to be late to class because his walk was too far. He failed to admit to himself that scores of other students had similar if not longer walks than he did yet they were able to make it to class on time.

By the time a student makes it to college teachers are not very interested in excuses as to why someone is constantly late. They don't much care about your personal life, your health, or how many times you are behind on assignments because of issues with your roommate or parents. Assignments need to be accomplished and there is very little room to fudge on grades. College and universities will always take your money, but they never guarantee a diploma.

Try this: Tell the truth and always start with yourself. Justification for one's actions is a slippery slope. Be honest with yourself and if you receive a poor grade on an assignment or project ask yourself if you truly gave it you best effort. The only person you can't lie to is yourself.

#5 When You Get Down - Get Busy

"One of the things I learned the hard way was that it doesn't pay to get discouraged. Keeping busy and making optimism a way of life can restore your faith in yourself."

Lucille Ball

I had a student in class recently who would get easily flustered when he got behind in his work. It was as if he couldn't focus on one task without worrying about another. He would get so frustrated that he would have trouble getting started because he was so wound up about being behind. We made a list of all the assignments he was missing. Once we had the work he needed to complete on paper I had him work on the assignment that required the least amount of effort. He was able to quickly check off one task from his list. This started the ball rolling and he was soon on his way to catching up while helping to lower his anxiety level.

Much like sport teams that experience some bad weeks in the course of a season, students will inevitably experience lulls in their performance during the long academic semester. The best teams will work hard to recognize what they need to do to get back on the winning track and take the steps required to correct problems and return to being successful. When good students, who typically get solid grades, fall behind they are willing to put in the extra work needed to get them back on track. These students will approach teachers about assignments and get any materials they may have missed. They have the drive to turn up their work production when they need it, and are willing and able to do so because they care about their grades and have previously developed the habit of completing work.

Failing students have gotten in the bad habit of throwing in the towel when they get behind in classes. Instead of pressuring themselves to get things accomplished they let themselves off the hook on completing work. Time and time again students fail - not because they are mentally inadequate - but because they are not willing to put forth the effort it takes to succeed.

Try this: If you find yourself behind in a class make a list of all the assignments and projects you are missing. Post the list in a place you can easily view and start working. Once you complete each assignment, cross it off your list until it is finished. Take the next step: See your teachers about any extra credit work.

#6 Take a Fun Class Each Semester

"He who laughs most learns best."
John Cleese

"Education is what remains after one has forgotten what one has learned in school."
Albert Einstein

While I was teaching a woodshop class to alternative education students who were struggling with grades, a boy told me, *"The only reason I come to school is because of this class."* His statement made me feel good, but it also made me realize the positive impact elective classes can have on children. This particular student was never great with academics, but he was good when it came to working with his hands. He went on to find success taking plumbing classes from our vocational school, a place that not only meet his interests but also gave him skills that he could apply to a career.

Not many things are as taxing as a full day of tough academic classes. A schedule that is filled with hard courses can make for a very difficult and not very enjoyable semester. It is important for students to take at least one class each semester that they look forward to because it is fun and enjoyable. These fun classes not only provide a break from traditional courses, but they also give students a chance to be exposed to subjects they typically know little about. Classes that are fun typically require less work outside of class, thus leaving students more time to concentrate on courses that have more homework.

Often students will discover educational interests while taking elective courses. Many students come to realize their strength in learning doesn't necessarily take place in traditional classroom settings taking core subjects, rather these passions are discovered in music, art, and vocational classes. With these interests piqued, students often get a clearer picture of the direction they may want to pursue with their future education and possible career choices.

Try this: Work with your counselor or adviser to develop a schedule next semester which includes a class that will be fun. Try not to schedule a course load that is completely filled with classes that will be difficult. Have a plan to have a class each semester that will be a break from the academic grind.

#7 Never Sell Yourself Short

"Everybody is a genius. But if you judge a fish by
its ability to climb a tree, it will live its whole life
believing that it is stupid."
Albert Einstein

I often get students who constantly belittled themselves and put themselves down. Their negativity can be
like a dark cloud above them that follows them around
and covers anyone who gets near them. These *'Debbie
Downers'* can be very difficult to be around because they
are always selling themselves short. Their attitude of focusing on their lack of success becomes a type of mantra
that turns into a self-fulfilling prophecy of inadequacy. In
short - stinking thinking produces smelly results.

Good students have a *'can do'* attitude about their
abilities. They are able to pick themselves up and rise to
the occasion through their will and desire to be successful.
They have learned to ignore adverse factors that arise in
one's life that can negatively impact a person's ability to
see themselves succeeding. They have learned to place
a high value on themselves. Rising above one's own
personal misgivings and doubts is perhaps the greatest
hurdle people face on the way to success and happiness.

A person's positive attitude towards their self-worth
is perhaps their greatest tool in achieving success and
overcoming obstacles. We can be very harsh and critical
of ourselves, but it is important to keep in mind that we
need to be our best ally as well. It is good for students to

learn from failures, but not to dwell on them. Academic success does not happen overnight. Build from your successes and grow your abilities while trusting and having faith in yourself to do well.

Try this: If you catch yourself cutting yourself down, stop! Turn the situation around and find a way to think about yourself in a positive way. Instead of saying, "I stink in math," say, "I've gotten better in math this year." Flip things around and put a positive spin on issues, and never cut yourself down.

#8 Don't Beat Yourself Up When You Fail

"I've missed more than 9000 shots in my career. I've lost almost 300 games. 26 times, I've been trusted to take the game winning shot and missed. I've failed over and over and over again in my life. And that is why I succeed."
Michael Jordan

I was watching the final round of a golf tournament recently and saw an experienced player completely fail on a hole in the middle of his round. He was in a water hazard, in a sand trap, and in some tall grass before he finally got his ball in the cup. Most players would get so flabbergasted from this failure that it would lead to a complete meltdown for the rest of their round. This player, however, was able to regroup from any negative thoughts and focus on the future holes in his round instead of dwelling on his past failure. He went on to shoot a very solid round, and although he did not win, he finished in the top ten.

Even the best students in school will experience failures; in class, with assignments, and on tests. These good students have learned that instead of beating themselves up when they fail it is better to recognize the reasons they did not succeed, and make adjustments so that in the future they will avoid the same mistakes. They don't take a bad grade as a reflection of any lack of character - rather they view a poor performance as a lack of proper preparation and they make corrections to see that it doesn't happen again.

The way we view our failures creates a mindset towards how we face future challenges. When poor students don't succeed they often view their lack of success as a failure in their personal character and they lack the confidence to have the ability to change. They view a failure as a type of confirmation of their inabilities to do well and they allow it to reinforce negative thoughts of any inadequacies they have. They beat themselves up and take to heart any failure as an extension of who they are. Unfortunately, for these students, self-deprecation and equating failure with self-worth is easily habit forming and only leads to more failure.

Try this: The next time you screw up an assignment or a test do an assessment of what happened. Ask yourself some questions such as: Did I study the right things for this test? Did I give myself plenty of time to prepare? Was I paying attention in class? Learn from your mistakes and move forward. Remember: *If we just experienced successes we wouldn't experience much joy.*

#9 Attack Your Weaknesses

"You cannot run away from weakness; you must some time fight it out or perish; and if that be so, why not now, and where you stand?"
Robert Louis Stevenson

I remember back in school it always seemed that I had at least one class each semester that was a type of thorn in my side. I would think to myself, *if I could just not be in this one class my grades and my semester would be much better.* I was slow to come to the realization that the best way to approach a difficult class was to attack the course with more effort.

If a basketball coach notices that his players are weak shooting foul shots he probably will not spend extra time in practice having his players concentrate on shooting layups. While shooting layups are fun, and relatively easy to make, they are not what the coach will want his players to practice. To become a better team while increasing their chances for success they will need to concentrate their efforts in areas of their game that they need to improve upon. Just as this team will need to spend more time shooting foul shots, students who are lacking at certain skills in school may need to work on those aspects to improve their education and their chances of succeeding.

Weak students have a tendency to put a low priority on work from classes they feel are difficult. They often approach hard subjects with dread, and as a result of this attitude, they give these classes less of their effort. Because of the level of commitment necessary to be successful in tough subjects are higher, many students will not put forth the time and work required and they end up falling behind, ultimately risking failure. While poor students will focus their efforts on easy subjects, the best students will recognize their areas of weakness and dedicate additional time and attention to these courses.

Try this: Pick the class that is giving you the most trouble and attack it with all your effort. Make this the class that is your first priority in doing homework. Attend any test review sessions that are offered. Ask clarification questions in class. Get tutoring help to guide you through more difficult lessons and concepts. Dedicate more time to this class and see how your efforts pay off.

#10 Think of School as an Opportunity to Learn

"A pessimist sees the difficulty in every opportunity; an optimist sees the opportunity in every difficulty."
Winston Churchill

"If opportunity doesn't knock, build a door."
Milton Berle

Most people will agree that education is our best chance to better ourselves. Our opportunity for advancement parallels our increase in our knowledge while giving us a chance to better our economic situation. The chart on the next page contains some recent data from the U. S. Department of Labor that illustrates the economic effects of getting an education.

Try this: Next time you feel discouraged about school, attempt to view your learning as a chance to increase your knowledge. Try to change your outlook on school work. See it as a chance to better your skills and increase your overall understanding. It pays to learn!

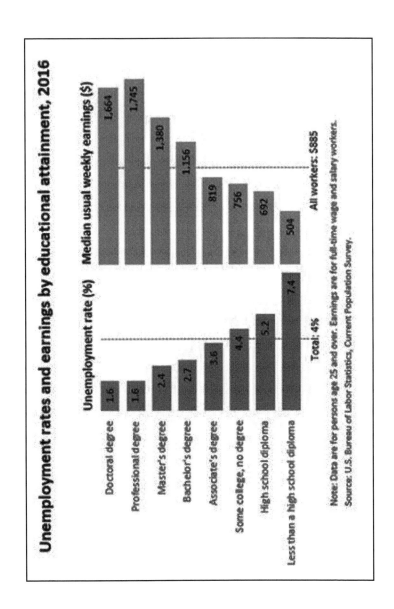

Unemployment rates and earnings by educational attainment, 2016

Median usual weekly earnings ($)

Education	Earnings
Doctoral degree	1,664
Professional degree	1,745
Master's degree	1,380
Bachelor's degree	1,156
Associate's degree	819
Some college, no degree	756
High school diploma	692
Less than a high school diploma	504

All workers: $885

Unemployment rate (%)

Education	Rate
Doctoral degree	1.6
Professional degree	1.6
Master's degree	2.4
Bachelor's degree	2.7
Associate's degree	3.6
Some college, no degree	4.4
High school diploma	5.2
Less than a high school diploma	7.4

Total: 4%

Note: Data are for persons age 25 and over. Earnings are for full-time wage and salary workers.
Source: U.S. Bureau of Labor Statistics, Current Population Survey.

#11 Be Your Own Hero - No One Else Will

"A hero is an ordinary individual who finds the strength to persevere and endure in spite of over-whelming obstacles."
Christopher Reeve

Lately the entertainment business has been producing films, video games, and stories that feature some type of super hero. While we have often had these types of characters in the past, comic book types of heroes have flooded the industry. It seems that through magic, special-ized abilities or some divine gifts most of today's heroes are able to solve their conflicts. Unfortunately we are mere mortals and a wave of a wand, a ring with powers, or x-ray vision just doesn't exist.

Good students come to realize that they are their best allies. As a student matures they begin to recognize the importance of doing things for themselves. They come to rely less on their parents and teachers to guide their deci-sions, while they seek out their own ways of approaching and solving obstacle they face. They become more of an actualized person that is self-reliant and responsible for their actions. These students evolve into leaders at their jobs and in their communities. They become the real heroes.

Some students rely much too heavily on help from others and fall into the trap of seeking help before they attempt to do things for themselves. I'm often asked by students about questions on tests, quizzes, and work-sheets. The first thing I do is ask them if they have read the directions. That direction from me usually takes care of the majority of problems they typically face. These students have learned that they can get the answers to their questions through methods other than having to think for themselves. While calculators, cell phones, and computers can be used as great tools for learning, they often serve as a type of crutch that enables students to bypass critical thinking in exchange for faster gratification.

Try this: Think of yourself as your personal super hero. If you want to achieve something remember that accomplishments must be self-generated. You cannot and should never expect others to help you reach your goals. It is always good to seek help when you need it, but you must be accountable for your achievements in life. Be your own hero, because as cool as superheroes are in the movies they don't exist in real life.

Last Thoughts

"One looks back with appreciation to the brilliant teachers, but with gratitude to those who touched our human feelings. The curriculum is so much necessary raw material, but warmth is the vital element for the growing plant and for the soul of the child."
Carl Jung

Growing up today is difficult because there are such a variety of attractive activities for kids to be drawn to. Unfortunately most of these distractions are more appealing than going to school and being a good student. Teachers are constantly trying to come up with innovative ways in which to capture the attention of students. Hopefully if parents and teachers can help students adopt some of the hints from this book young people can start to navigate through all the distractors that impede their learning.

While I feel these hints are important for a child to learn to be better at school they are far from the most important thing. Without adults making positive connections with students these hints lose influence and in the mind of some students they become just another part of learning they don't want to know. For teachers and parents to be effective it is truly about building relationships with kids through developing trust and good role modeling. So many kids lose interest in a class and fail if they develop a conflict with their instructor. If educators strive to develop a rapport with their students it can often become their best asset when attempting to teach them the content of lessons as well as hints that help them be more successful at school.

Try this: Attempt to find out something new about each of your students.

About the Author

Joe Deely graduated with a Masters in Education degree from James Madison University in 1995 and started teaching that fall. He has taught students in grades 6 through 12 his entire 23-year career in public schools.

As an alternative education teacher, he finds that his students often struggle with academic, social, and emotional difficulties. His specialty is teaching kids who have a hard time understanding what to do to be successful at school.

"I learn something every day from my students that helps me become a better teacher," he notes, adding, "The lessons they have taught me have inspired this book."

82167591R00087

Made in the USA
Columbia, SC
14 December 2017